Sarada Prasad Sarkar

Students History of Bengal

Sarada Prasad Sarkar

Students History of Bengal

ISBN/EAN: 9783337385286

Printed in Europe, USA, Canada, Australia, Japan

Cover: Foto ©ninafisch / pixelio.de

More available books at **www.hansebooks.com**

STUDENT'S HISTORY OF BENGAL

BY

SARADA PRASAD SARKAR

DEPUTY MAGISTRATE AND DEPUTY COLLECTOR,
AUTHOR OF 'EXAMPLES IN ARITHMETIC,' 'ELEMENTS OF ARITHMETIC
IN BENGALI,' ETC. ETC.

WITH A MAP OF BENGAL

HARE PRESS:—CALCUTTA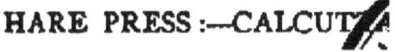

1888

PREFACE.

HAVING been entrusted with the management of a school, it struck me while selecting text books for the various classes, that the first history which should fall in the hands of the little boys of our Anglo-Bengali schools, ought to be a history of Bengal. The pupils should read the history of their own country, before commencing that of a foreign nation. There are many things in the history of Bengal that are of some import to the future life of a child, things independent of the change of kings or the fighting of battles.

PREFACE.

Finding that a proper history of Bengal for the young boys of our schools is a *desideratum*, I have undertaken the compilation of this little book. I have kept in view that the history should neither be too much elementary in its character nor too much overcrowded with facts; that it should be simple and interesting.

I have laboriously tried to collect the facts from the best authentic sources; and attempted to treat them in a way to engage the attention and fix them in the memory so that the study of larger treatises by them later on may be rendered easier.

The labours and researches of many eminent writers and antiquarians, such as Dr. Buchanon Hamilton, Dr. Rajendra Lal Mittra, Sir William Hunter, Mr. E. V. Westmacott, Professor Blochman, Babus Kissori Chand Mittra, Bhawani Charan Bandyopadhyay, Rajkrishna Mukhopadhyay and others have thrown a flood of light on the obscure period of Bengal history. The materials obtained from their writings I have made the basis of the Hindu period.

In compiling the Muhammadan and English periods, I have freely availed myself of the materials derived from the various reports published by Government, and from the admirable Statistical Account of Bengal by Sir William Hunter. I have consulted also the works of Professor Blochman, Mr. Toynbee, Rev. J. Long, Dr. Marshman, Mr. Stewart, Sir J.W. Kaye, Captain Lewin, Captain Macpherson and many others.

The history of Bengal is replete with facts to teach the young pupils the lessons of loyalty, and that the happiness of a country mainly depends upon a settled government. If I have succeeded in teaching them to love their own country, and to honor and respect the Government which has conferred upon it innumerable benefits, all I have aimed at will be attained.

In conclusion, I beg to express my great obligations to my friends Babus Rajani Kanta Rai, B. A. and Srigopal Chatterjea, M. A. for the help they have rendered in my offering this little book to the public, and to Lieut.-Colonel J. Waterhouse, B. S. C., for his kind permission to have the Map of Bengal lithographed in the Surveyor-General's Office.

S. P. SARKAR.

MANICKGANJ : *June*, 1888.

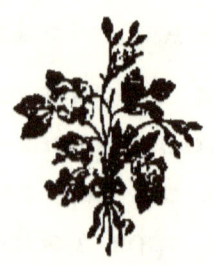

CONTENTS.

CHAPTER.   PAGE.
- I. The Physical Features of Bengal.—Its area, climate, chief staples and census . 1
- II. The Present Civil Divisions of Bengal and Forms of Administration. . . . 9
- III. Banga Des.—Its people. 12
- IV. Ancient Kingdoms of Bengal. . . . 25
- V. The Muhammadan Conquest of Bengal. . 40
- VI. Dependent Pathan Kings of Bengal. . 43
- VII. Independent Pathan Kings of Bengal. . 49
- VIII. The Mughal Subadars of Bengal. . . 66
- IX. The Nawabs-Nazim of Bengal. . . . 87
- X. The Company's Nawabs of Bengal. . . 111
- XI. The Company Bahadur's Rule in Bengal. . 122
  - Sec. I. The Administration of Governors-General.
  - Sec. II. The Administration of Lieutenant-Governor.
- XII. The Rule of the British Crown. . . 166

STUDENT'S
HISTORY OF BENGAL.

CHAPTER I.

THE PHYSICAL FEATURES OF BENGAL.—ITS AREA, CLIMATE, CHIEF STAPLES AND CENSUS.

Boundaries.—Bengal includes the four great provinces of Bengal Proper, Behar, Orissa, and Chutiá Nágpur, and is bounded on the north by Bhutan and Nepal; on the east by Assam and the mountainous region of Northern Burma; on the south by the Bay of Bengal, Madras and the Central Provinces; and on the west by the North-Western Provinces and the Central India.

Area.—Its area is 150,588 square miles exclusive of the area of large rivers and of the Sunderbans, which is estimated to be 5,976 square miles. Besides the above under direct British rule, there are territories governed by semi-independent chiefs. These are the principalities of Kuch Behar and Hill Tipperah, situated respectively on the north-eastern and eastern boundaries of Bengal. There are also two groups of petty states which lie to the south and south-west of the province. They are the Tributary States of Orissa and of Chutiá Nágpur. The area of these territories is 36,634 square miles. The area of whole Bengal may therefore be stated to be 193,198 square miles, including the Sunderbans.

Rivers.—The *Ganges* enters Lower Bengal near Gázipur; shortly after, it receives Gogra on the north bank, the Son on the south, and the Gandak again on the north, at Hájipur. The Kusi joins it below Bhagalpur; after which the river turns the corner of the Rajmahal hills and assumes a southerly direction, till the Bhagirati flows away to the west to form the Hugli, and the main stream continues south-east to Goalanda, where the Jamuna, the principal branch of the Brahmaputra, is met. About 220 miles from its mouth, the Ganges spreads out into numerous branches, forming a delta. The navigable streams which fall into the Ganges intersect the country in every direction and afford abundant facilities for internal communication. The lower region of the Ganges is the richest and most productive portion of Bengal, and abounds in valuable produce.

The *Brahmaputra* is formed by the union of several great streams. It flows towards the south-west through the length of the Assam valley; after which it turns round the Garo Hills and then proceeds due southwards to its junction with the Ganges near Goalanda.

The *Feni*, which separates Tipperah and Noakhali from Chittagong falls into the east of the Bay of Bengal. The *Karnafuli*, on which Chittagong is situated, rises in the north-east of the Chittagong Hill Tracts and after a westerly and south-westerly course falls into the Bay of Bengal. Its principal tributary is the Halda. The *Sangu* after a very circuitous course also enters the Bay ten miles south of Karnafuli.

The rivers of the western side of the Gangetic delta have little or no connection with the main water system of the country. The *Damudah*, the *Rupnarain* and the *Kansabati* or *Kansai* all join the Hugli between Calcutta and Sagar Island. They have sprung from the plateau of Chutiá Nágpur.

The *Hugli* is the most westerly, and for commercial purposes the most important channel, by which the Ganges enters the Bay of Bengal. It takes its distinctive name near the town of Santipur, a little above the point, where the *Bhagirati* joins the *Matabhanga* at a distance of about 120 miles from the sea. The stream thus formed, represents three western distributaries of the Ganges— (1) the *Bhagirati*, (2) the *Jalangi*, and (3) the part of the *Matabhanga* which branches off in the Nadiya district. Proceeding south from Santipur it divides Murshidabad from the Hugli district, until it touches the district of 24 Parganahs. It then proceeds almost due south to Calcutta, next bends to south-west, and finally turns south, entering the Bay.

The *Subarnarekhá*, the *Baitarani* and the *Mahanadi* of Orissa, have a direction generally parallel to one another, and a south-easterly course. The two former rise in

Chutiá Nágpur and the latter rises in the Central Provinces.

The Mohananda, which passes through the Darjiling district, is a small stream, and loses itself in the sand of the Terái.

Mountains.—The *Himálayan* Chain vary in elevation from Darjiling, 7,167 ft. above sea-level to lofty Kinchinjinga, 28,000 ft. high.

Sinchál is a long undulating range of hills in the Darjiling district. The main peak is 8,607 feet above sea-level. Its summits are locally known as the *Bara* and *Chota Durbin*.

The *Sinchulía* range in the Jalpiguri district forms the boundary between British territory and Bhutan.

The *Rajmahal* hills cover an area of 1,366 square miles, from the borders of Central India to the town of Rajmahal round which the Ganges flows.

To the south of Chutiá Nágpur, on the west side of Orissa, are the Orissa Tributary Mahals, a hilly country containing forests of *sál*.

The principal hill ranges in the Chittagong district are (1) the *Sitakunda*, (2) the *Golias*, (3) the *Satkania*, (4) the *Maskhal*, and (5) the *Teknaf*. Of these the most interesting is the first named, containing the sacred peak of *Chandranath*, 1,155 feet in height.

Hill Tipperah and the Chittagong Hill Tracts are mountainous regions to the east of Bengal. The highest peak in Hill Tipperah is 3,200 feet above sea-level. Dense forests cover the whole of these hilly tracts. The highest hills in the Chittagong Hill Tracts are *Rang-rang-dang* (2789 ft.) and *Lurain-Tang* (2,355 feet). The majority of the inhabitants of these tracts are either Chakmas or Maghs, both of which races profess the Buddhist religion.

Plains.—The greater part of Bengal and Behar consists of uninterrupted flats, subject to inundation. The Dacca division is so fertile that it has been called the granary of Bengal. If a line be drawn southwards between Bankura and Bardwan, and carried on past Mednipur and down towards Balasor, it will be noticed that to the west, the ground partakes of the character of the Chutiá Nágpur plateau, granite being found overlaid with sandstone containing iron and coal in great abundance.

Lakes.—The *Chilka* lake is situated in the south-east corner of the Puri district in Orissa. It is 44 miles long and has a mean breadth of 20 miles in its northern half and about 5 miles in the southern. Its area is 344 square miles, increasing to about 450 during the rainy season. The average depth is from 3 to 5 feet and nowhere it exceeds 6 feet.

The *Salt Water Lake* in the district of 24 Parganahs is five miles east of Calcutta between the Hugli and Bidhyadhari rivers and covers an area of about 30 square miles. A part of the lake is in course of reclamation by the sewage of Calcutta being deposited in it.

The most remarkable *jhils* are in Rajshahi, Jessore and Bakargang.

Climate.—*Temperature.*—Although the Province of Bengal is situated almost entirely without the tropical Zone its climate is characteristically tropical.

Humidity.—The high humidity of the atmosphere in Bengal has become proverbial. The absolute humidity of the atmosphere is greatest on the coast of Orissa and the Sunderbans, and diminishes inland as the distance from the sea increases.

Rain-fall.—The districts of Eastern Bengal and the Himalayan Terái are those of the heaviest rain-fall. The lowest rain-fall in the provinces is that of the central and southern portions of Behar, including the Monghyr, Gya, Patna, and Saran districts where the annual fall very slightly exceeds 40 inches.

Food Grains.—*Rice* is the principal article of food among the Bengalis. There are many varieties of rice; but the crop is divided into two main species—*aus* or early and *aman* or winter rice. Another main species is the *boro* or spring rice. *Aman* is of two kinds, *chhátán* and *boran*. *Chhátán* or early *aman* is the best sort of rice and is known as *ruyá* or transplanted *dhán*. *Boran aman* is a coarser sort of rice and is known as *bond* or sown. The average out-turn of rice per acre, may be taken at 15 *máns*. The districts of the whole of Bengal Proper and the Province of Orissa (an area of about one hundred thousand square miles) constitute the rice producing area.

Wheat is an important food staple in Behar. Bhagalpur is the chief wheat producing district of Behar, and next comes Monghyr. The only districts from which wheat is exported from Bengal are Nadiya and Murshidabad.

Murwa and *Kodo* are both cheaper than rice, and are much eaten by the lower classes in Gya and in the Chutiá Nágpur division.

Barley is generally eaten in the form of *chhátu* with salt and chillies. Throughout Behar it is one of the cheapest food crops.

Makái that is maize or Indian corn is the cheapest of all food grains. It is prepared and eaten like barley. In Patna and Shahabad, it is consumed even more than barley by the labouring classes.

Chiná and *kdon* are largely cultivated and consumed in Behar and Chutiá Nágpur. *Vuhra* is a coarse grain seed eaten by the poorer classes.

Dal or pulses are a most important food staple throughout the whole of Bengal and Behar. The principal pulses are *Matar, Khesari, Mushuri, Maskalai, Mug, But* or *Chhola,* and *Arhur.*

Commercial Staples.—Jute or *pat* or *kosta* grows well in Bengal on almost every description of soil. *San* or a kind of hemp is grown for fibres. Its chief local use is the manufacture of nets and cordage for boats. *Dhanchi* or *Dhancha* is a hardier plant than jute. *Ganja* is real hemp whose leaves are smoked and cause intoxication. Its seeds produce oil which is used for lamps and in the manufacture of soap, paints and varnishes. In Rajshahi the seeds are baked and eaten as an article of food but not extensively. *Mashina* or linseed is extensively cultivated for its oil. Damp districts are not well suited for this plant. *Mustard seed* is extensively cultivated and consumed by the people. *Cotton* is not produced in any of the districts of Bengal; except in Chittagong and Tipperah Hill Tracts, Cuttack and parts of Jalpiguri. *Sugar* is manufactured both from sugarcane and date tree. The cultivation of the date tree and the manufacture of date sugar are extensively carried on in the districts of Faridpur, Bhagalpur, Jessore, in parts of Nadiya, the 24 Parganahs and Khulna. The sugarcane of which there are several varieties, is grown throughout the Province. It is most extensively cultivated in the Patna, Rajshahi and Kuch Behar and Bardwan divisions. *Tobacco* is grown more or less extensively in every district in Bengal. It is grown in Rangpur, Dinajpur, Darbhanga, Purniah, 24 Parganahs, the Chittagong Hill Tracts and Nadiya for trade and export. *Tea* is cultivated in Rajshahi and Kuch Behar, Chittagong, Dacca, and Chutiá Nágpur divisions. *Indigo* is grown in the districts of Nadiya and Jessore, and throughout Central Bengal, in Purniah, and westward in all Behar north of the Ganges. *Opium* is grown and manufactured in the valley of the Ganges round Patna and Benares.

Silk was once a very important industry in Bengal but it is fast declining. The manufacture of silk is carried on chiefly in parts of the Bardwan division, and in the districts of Rajshahi, Murshidabad, Maldah and the Santhal Parganahs. *Lac* or *(lah)* is manufactured in the districts of Lohardagga and Manbhum in the Chutiá Nágpur division and in the Bankura and Birbhum districts in the Bardwan division.

Saltpetre is a chief industry in the districts of Mazafarpur, Darbhanga, Saran, and Champaran. *Cinchona*, the cultivation of which was introduced as an experiment in a valley of the Himalayas in the district of Darjiling has proved a great success.

Census.—The total population of the Province under the Lieutenant-Governor of Bengal is nearly 7 *krors*. They are distributed into Hindus, Muhammadans, Buddhists, Christians, Brahmos, Sikhs, Jains, Jews, Parsis and many aboriginal tribes. The Muhammadans number about 2 *krors*, 17 *laks;* the Hindus about 4½ *krors;* the Buddhists about 1½ *laks;* the Christians about 1¼ *laks;* and the Santals, Kols, and other aborigines about 21 *laks.*

Of the various languages Bengali is the mother-tongue of 3 *krors* and 64 *laks;* Hindi, Hindustani, and Urdu are spoken by about 2 *krors*, 48 *laks;* and Uriya by about 54½ *laks.* The Kolarian languages, Santali, Kol, Manda, and Bhil are spoken by 21½ *laks;* while English is stated to be the mother-tongue of about 37½ thousand persons.

CHAPTER II.

THE PRESENT CIVIL DIVISIONS OF BENGAL AND FORMS OF ADMINISTRATION.

Civil Divisions.—The Province is divided into :—

(1) Regulation Districts, that is districts subject to the general regulations and Acts.

(2) Non-regulation Districts, that is districts to which the regulations and Acts do not apply of their own force but to which they may be extended at the discretion of government.

(3) Semi-independent and Tributary States, administered or partly administered by British officers.

CLASS I.—The districts under the first and second heads are grouped together and formed into divisions for purposes of administration, over each of which divisions there is a Commissioner of Revenue. They are—

I. 1. 24 Parganahs, 2. Nadiya, 3. Jessore, 4. Murshidabad, 5. Khulna forming the Presidency Division.

II. 1. Bardwan, 2. Bankura, 3. Birbhum, 4. Hugli, 5. Mednipur forming the Bardwan Division.

III. 1. Rajshahi, 2. Dinajpur, 3. Rangpur, 4. Bagura, 5. Pubna, 6. Darjiling, 7. Jalpiguri, forming the Rajshahi and Kuch Behar Division.

IV. 1. Dacca, 2. Faridpur, 3. Bakarganj, 4. Maimansing forming the Dacca Division.

V. 1. Chittagong, 2. Noakhali, 3. Tipperah forming the Chittagong Division.

VI. 1. Monghyr, 2. Bhagalpur, 3. Purniah, 4. Maldah, 5. Santal Parganahs forming the Bhagalpur Division.

VII. 1. Patna, 2. Gya, 3. Shahabad, 4. Mazafarpur, 5. Darbhanga, 6. Saran, 7. Champaran forming the Patna Division.

VIII. 1. Cuttack, 2. Puri, 3. Balasor forming the Orissa Division.

IX. 1. Hazaribagh, 2. Lohardagga, 3. Manbhum, 4. Singbhum forming the Chutiá Nágpur Division.

CLASS II. Under the second head come the Santal Parganahs and the Hill Tracts of Chittagong, which are still administered under a peculiar system, and the districts of Jalpiguri, Darjiling, Hazaribag, Lohardagga, Manbhum, and Singbhum, in which many of the general laws are at present in force.

CLASS III. Under the third head are the Tributary Mahals of Orissa and Chutiá Nágpur.

Executive Administration.—Each district is under

the control of a District Officer, who is styled Magistrate-Collector in the regulation districts and Deputy Commissioner in the non-regulation districts. At the disposal of the District Officer are the subordinate magisterial, police and revenue authorities. The District Superintendent of Police is the head of the police force under the Magistrate. The Sub-divisional Officers, who are Assistant or Deputy Magistrates in charge of divisions of districts, exercise in their own jurisdictions the delegated power of the District Officer, except in matters of police over which they have only judicial and no executive control.

Above the District Magistrates are the Divisional Commissioners. Their duties are principally those of supervision. In the Revenue Department they keep a control over the Collectors' proceedings. The Commissioners are in their turn, subject to the orders of the Board of Revenue in revenue matters; in other matters they are under the government direct. The Lieutenant-Governor is the head of the Bengal Government. He possesses complete authority in all the departments of the Civil Administration. He has a Council to make laws and Acts.

Revenue Administration.—The revenues of the Province are derived from the following sources:—the land revenue, the monopoly of opium, excise on spirits and intoxicating drugs, stamps, salt, income-tax, and the Public Works Cess. Of these, land revenue, excise, stamps and the income taxes are managed by the District Collectors, but the opium, customs and salt revenue are under special departments. The opium branch is under the management of two Opium Agents. At the head of the Customs is a special Collector. The District Collector is controlled by the Revenue Commissioner, who again is subject to the orders of the Members of the Board of Revenue. The Board consists of two members who are each the heads of their own Departments. The Senior Member is in charge of Land Revenue, and the Junior has charge of all other sources of revenue.

Criminal Administration.—Criminal justice is administered by the High Court, the Courts of Session, and the Courts of the various classes of Magistrates.

Civil Administration.—In respect of civil justice, the High Court exercises an appellate, a legal and equitable jurisdiction. Below the High Court are the District and Additional Judges, the Small Cause Court and Subordinate Judges, and the Munsiffs.

CHAPTER III.

BANGA DES.—ITS PEOPLE.

The Aborigines.—The oldest dwellers in Bengal consisted of many tribes whom the victorious Aryans described as *Dasyus, Rakhases, Pisaches, &c.* They were the primitive tribes, who, in the absence of a race name of their own, are called non-Aryans or Aborigines. The Vedic hymns abound in phrases describing them as 'disturbers of sacrifices,' 'feeders on flesh,' 'raw eaters,' 'without gods,' 'without rites,' and many other scornful epithets. When the lordly Aryans settled in the land, they either drove them back to the mountains or reduced them to servitude on the plains. Many of these primitive tribes exist at the present day each with its own set of curious customs and religious rites. Some are still in the same early stage of human creation, while others have made advances in social progress. The principal of them may be found in the hills lying in the Eastern frontier, in the Santal Parganahs, in Chutiá Nágpur and Hazaribag, and in the Tributary States of Orissa.

The Hill Tribes* of Chittagong Hill Tracts.—The tribes inhabiting the Hill Tracts of Chittagong are divided into two classes :—(1) the Khyoungtha, or Children of the River, who are of Arakanese origin, speak the ancient Arakan dialect, and follow the Buddhist religion and customs; and (2) the Toungtha, or Children of the Hills, who are either aborigines or of mixed origin, speak different dialects and are purely savages.

The *Khyoungtha* or Jumia † Maghs as they are called, live in village communities, having a *roaja* or village head; The position of *roaja* is more an honorable than a profitable one. He is chosen by the villagers, and appointed by the chief. The *roaja* decides all petty cases and disputes in the village. Before their conversion to Buddhism they worshipped the spirits of the hills and streams. The dress of the Khyoungtha is simple. The men wear a home-made cloth reaching below the knee. Around the bosom of the women is wound a cloth about a span wide, the arms and neck being exposed.

---

* For an elaborate account see 'The Hill Tracts of Chittagong and the Dwellers therein' by Capt. Lewin.

† *Jum* is the hill mode of cultivation.

The parents look about for some young girl to marry his son, unless, as is more often the case, he has fixed upon a partner himself. The Khyoungtha burn their dead. Their written character is the same as the Burmese. Their mode of salutation is strange; they apply the mouth and nose to the cheek and give a strong inhalation. They do not say "give me a kiss" but "smell me."

Of the *Toungtha* tribes, some are entirely under British control; and some are entirely independent. They are the Lushais or Kukis who are more purely savages, and unamenable to civilization. Their villages are generally situated on lofty hills and are difficult of access. The men wear scarcely any clothing, and the petticoat of women is scanty, reaching only to the knee. Both men and women are given to dancing together. Upon the women falls the greater part of the labour of life. Their religion is simple; it is the religion of nature; they worship the terrene elements. Reverence or respect are emotions unknown to them; they salute neither their chiefs nor their elders; no form of greeting exists in their many tongues, neither have they any expression conveying thanks. They attach importance to an oath, which is made upon the things on which their very existence may be said to depend—namely water, cotton, rice and the *dáo*. Slavery is common; but the bond people are universally treated well.

Hill Tribes of Hill Tipperah.—The hill tribes of Hill Tipperah are (1) the Tipperahs, (2) the Hallams, (3) the Kukis, and (4) the Manipuris.

The Tipperahs.—The Tipperahs are all of the same religion, and speak the same language, differing only in minor local peculiarities. They worship the elements, such as the god of water, the god of fire, the god of forests, the god of earth &c. Sacrifices form an important part of their religion; buffaloes, pigs, goats, and fowls being the animals ordinarily used for the purpose. Like all the hill tribes, the village community is governed by the headmen. The Tipperahs are passionately fond of dancing and at the time of their great harvest festival in November the dances are kept up sometimes for two days and two nights without intermission. At a marriage there is no particular ceremony but a good deal of feasting and dancing. A Tipperah widow may remarry. Divorce may be obtained among the Tipperahs, as among all the hill tribes, on the adjudication of a jury of village elders. When a Tipperah dies, his body is burned at the waterside.

The *Hallams.*—They are of Kuki origin. Their language is a mere dialect of Kuki, and a Kuki and a Hallam can readily understand each other. The customs of the Hallams are becoming more closely allied with those of the Tipperahs. The Hallams and Tipperahs can live in the same village, so can Kukis and Hallams, but not Kukis and Tipperahs.

The *Kukis.*—The Kukis of Hill Tipperah are of the same race as the Lushais, who live further to the east and who call themselves Kachha Kukis. They belong to the same class whose accounts we have given already.

The *Manipuris.*—Colonel Dalton clearly connects the present race with the Nagas and the Kukis. The valley was at first occupied by several tribes, but by degrees the Meithei became dominant, and that name was applied to the entire colony. They have now adopted the Hindu faith and they claim to be of Hindu descent. Colonel M'Culloch fixes the date of the adoption of Hinduism by the Manipuris in A. D. 1714.

The Santals.—The Santals are found in the Districts of Bhagalpur, the Santal Parganahs, Birbhum, Bankura, Hazaribagh, Manbhum, Medinipur, Singbhum, Morbhunj, and Balasor.

In each Santal village there is (1) a *Jagmanjhi* whose most important duty is apparently to look after the morals of the boys and girls; (2) a *Paramanik* whose business is to attend to the farming arrangements, and to apportion the lands; (3) a *Naiya* or village priest. Ancestors are worshipped, or rather their memory is honored, and offerings made at home by each head of a family. The Santals are not over-particular about food, but nothing will induce them to eat rice cooked by a Hindu, or even by a Brahman.

An eldest son is always named after his grandfather; other children after other relations. The Santals have adopted as a rite the tonsure of children. Child marriage is not practised. Utmost liberty is given to the youth of both sexes. The old people, though affecting great regard for the honor of the girls, display great confidence in their virtue. Unrestrained, they resort to markets, to festivals, and village dances in groups. The Santals have a proficiency in flute made of bamboo. In front of the *Jagmanjhi's* house there is a dancing place, where the young men and women frequently resort after the evening meal. A peculiar ceremony is observed during a Santal marriage and no priest officiates at it. At the close of the ceremony tne young people are thus admonished by one of the sages :—'oh boy ! oh girl ! you are from this day forth to comfort each other in sickness or sorrow. Hitherto you have only played and worked, now the responsibility of the household duties is upon you, practise hospitality, and when a kinsman arrives wash his feet and respectfully salute him.' In prosperous seasons a Santal is either busy with his cultivation, or playing his flute or dancing with the girls, or engaged in the chase. They solemnly burn their dead, and float three fragments of the skull down the Damodar river, the sacred stream of the race.

The Kandhs* of Orissa.—The aboriginal and semi-aboriginal hill tribes of the Tributary States of Orissa, are most numerous in the mountainous jungles of Morbhunj, Keunjhar and Bod.

The word 'Kandh' in the aboriginal languages, means 'mountaineer.' As the Hindu Rajas drove them deeper into the recesses of the hills, the tribe split up into three sections. The weaker of them remained as a landless low caste in the new Hindu principalities; another class obtained military tenures, and formed a peasant militia such as that which again and again beat back the wave of Musalman conquest from Orissa; the third wrung from their Hindu neighbours the position and the privileges of free allies.

In each family among the Kandhs the absolute authority rests with the house father. The sons have no property

---

* Lieutenant Macpherson's Report is a great storehouse of facts with regard to the Kandhs in their primitive state.

during their father's lifetime; and all the male children, with their wives and descendants, continue to share the father's meal, prepared by the common mother. The patriarchal authority forms the basis of the social structure of the Kandhs. They make the patriarchal office hereditary as to family, but elective as to person. The eldest son of the patriarchal family has a prior title to the post; but if his character unfit him for its duties, he makes way for an younger brother or an uncle. The Kandh patriarch is the Father, the Magistrate, and the High priest of his people. He receives no pay, nor any official privileges other than the respect and veneration which belong to him. He leads in war; at home he is the protector of public order and the arbiter of private wrongs.

Before the English introduced milder laws, disputes among the Kandhs were settled by duels or by deadly combats. In case of murder, the duty fell upon the male kindred to kill the slayer. But the custom of blood-revenge was modified by the principle of money compensation. Offences against the person might be made amends for by compensation in property; and the sufferer had a right to live at the cost of his assailant until perfectly recovered. No payment could wipe out the stain of adultery. The injured husband was bound to put to death an adulterer, and to send back his wife to her father's house. In offences against property the principle of restitution reigned supreme. A stolen article must be returned, or its equivalent must be paid. A repetition of the crime made the criminal liable to be expelled from his tribe.

The right to the soil arises from priority of occupation. Kandh tillage still retains some of the migratory features common to the nomadic husbandry of most aboriginal tribes. When a piece of land shows signs of exhaustion, they abandon it and they change their villages once in about fourteen years.

The law of inheritance among the Kandhs is that the agricultural stock and landed property descend exclusively in the male line. On failure of sons, they go to the father's brothers, as women are deemed incapable to hold real property. The daughters divide among themselves the personal ornaments, money and moveable property of their deceased father, and have a right to maintenance from their brothers while they remain single, together with the expenses of their marriage.

The Kandh celebrates birth, marriage and death with ceremonies and solemnities all his own. A Kandh boy marries when he reaches his tenth or twelfth year. His wife is usually about four years older or about fifteen. The bridegroom's father pays a price for the bride; and she remains almost as a servant in her father-in-law's house until her boy-husband reaches a fit age to live with her. Women hold a high position among the Kandhs. On the death of a Kandh, his kinsmen quickly burn the body, and on the tenth day give a drinking feast to the hamlet.

Every Kandh tills his own land, and heartily despises all who follow any occupation save agriculture and war. Each Kandh hamlet has certain servile castes belonging to it. A few families of hereditary weavers (Pans), iron-smiths (Lohars), potters (Kumbhars), herdsmen (Gairs), and distillers (Sunris) hang about the outskirts of the village. A Kandh, eating food prepared by their hands, and engaging in any of their occupations brings disgrace upon himself.

The single vice of the Kandhs is drunkenness; and while drunkenness is held to be a laudable custom among the men, in women it is rare and would be deemed disgraceful.

The Kandhs believe in many terrible gods who dwell upon the earth and under the earth, in the waters and in the sky, each and all of whom must be propitiated by victims. One great ceremony which united the whole Kandh race is the worship of the Earth-God and human sacrifice formed an indispensable part of the public worship of the Kandhs. As soon as the Kandh tribes passed under the British rule, the practice was put down. To Lieutenant S. C. Macpherson belongs the credit of extirpating the rite.

The Aryans.—According to the *Sástras* or Sacred Books, the Hindu Aryans or Sanskrit speaking race first settled in the Panjab and the North-Western Provinces, to the west of the river Saraswati and northward of the Vindhya Mountains. It is impossible to historically trace their diffusion into Bengal, then said to be inhabited by aborigines called *Kírats*. According to the *Purans*, Banga, Sunma and Pundra, remote descendants of Jajati, the celebrated king of the lunar race were the first immigrants into Eastern India and the name Bengal or *Banga Des* is traditionally derived from Banga. The tract of country described by these three names does not extend further south than a portion of Nadiya. It is impossible however to fix the period when the Aryans arrived, although the Bengal immigration probably took place prior to Alexander's invasion.

Castes.—The existence of a large number of castes, into which the population has now become divided, is thus accounted for by the *Purans*. In the Golden age reigned a king named Bana, who taught his subjects that the precepts of the Vedas were unfounded; that heavenly bliss consisted of earthly enjoyment, and that death was utter annihilation. Hitherto there had only been four grand divisions among the people, who could not intermarry with each other. Bana, in order to increase the population, sanctioned promiscuous marriages among all classes. After Bana's death, the offspring of these marriages were aranged into classes or castes by his successor Prithu. He assigned different occupations to the various castes, and many of the castes up to the present day, have confined themselves to their hereditary employment.

The Brahmans.—The Vaidik Brahmans formed the original priestly class of this part of the country. They emigrated from Orissa, before the arrival of the five Brahmans from Oudh. According to one account, it was in consequence of their refusal to act as sacrificial priests to king Adisur, on the ground of his not being a Brahman, that that monarch brought down the five Brahmans from Kanauj. The other account says that the Brahmans who first settled in Bengal, had gradually given up the study of the Sacred Law and become degraded, and in consequence of this the five Brahmans were imported. In the twelfth century king Ballal Sen divided them into classes. The other Brahmans are merely descendants of immigrants from the different parts of India. Many of the Brahmans have lapsed from their high rank, and lost the esteem which the name commands, by indiscriminately accepting alms or by ministering as priests to the low castes.

The Kshattriyas.—The Kshattriyas formed the second or warrior caste in the ancient Sanskrit social fourfold classification, but it is believed that no pure Kshattriyas exist in Bengal Proper at the present day. Several of the tribes of the North-Western Provinces, such as the Rajputs and Marwari or up-country trading caste lay claim to the rank of Kshattriyas.

The Baidyas.—The Baidyas or physicians come next. A Hindu legend relates that Garar Muni, a sage of ancient times, was much surprised at finding his cottage cleaned out every morning, without being able to discover by whom. Accordingly, one day he hid himself, and saw a Vaisya girl enter the cottage and set it in order. The sage then came forward, and blessed her, and wished she might have a son. The girl was unmarried, but the words of the holy man once spoken could not be recalled. In due time she gave birth to a son, called Amritacharya. He married the daughter of Aswini-kumar, the physician of the gods, and the modern Baidyas are said to be his descendants. The popular belief, however, is that they were the offspring of a Brahman father and a Vaisya mother.

The Kayasthas.—The ancestors of the modern Kayasthas are said to have come as servants to the five Brahmans brought from Kanauj by king Adisur. The Kayasthas of Bengal Proper, the Karans of Orissa, and the Lala Kayets of Upper India, are, according to the old caste classification, writers or clerks. In Bengal proper they hold a position higher than Sudras but lower than the Brahmans. The Kayasthas deny that they are Sudras and assert that they originated from the *kayá* or body of Brahma, the Creator. From Brahma came Pradip Muni, who had three sons, Chittragupta, Chitrangada and Seni, the last of whom is claimed to be the original ancestor of the Kayasthas on this earth. As a matter of fact, they probably derived their origin from the upper classes of the people. Wealth, influence, and pretension to learning separated them, and formed them into a distinct caste. Many of them lay claim to the rank of Kshattriyas but such claim to higher rank is common with the lower classes. Thus the Dravidian Kochs believe themselves to be the descendants of Kshattriyas. The Mongolian Manipuris assert themselves to be the descendants of Arjun. The aboriginal Kacharis got themselves proclaimed to be the descendants of Bhim. The Kayastha was not one of the castes established by Manu. Perhaps society had not been sufficiently developed in his time to require a separate writer class.

Sudra Castes.—Following the Kayasthas come the undoubted Sudras, who comprise the large portion of the Hindu population, and are divided into many castes, sub-divided into many classes. The Sudra castes were originally nine in number, called *nabasaks* but some of them have split up into many sub-divisions; in other cases lower castes have by their wealth and importance, succeeded in forcing themselves into a higher social position than that properly belonging to their caste. Generally these Sudra castes are divided into three classes :—Pure Sudras, Intermediate Sudras and Low Sudras.

Semi-Aboriginal Castes.—Many castes appear to be semi-aborigines, who have been brought, in the course of time, within the pale of Hinduism. They form the very lowest of the Sudra castes and are utterly despised; such as Behara, Dulia, Chandal, Dom, Dhoba, Kaora, Muchi, Chamar, &c.

Threefold division of the Hindus.—Thus the present Hindu population of Bengal consists of (1) the Aborigines or non-Aryans; (2) the Aryans chiefly the Brahmans; (3) the mixed Hindus of Aryan and non-Aryan extraction.

The Muhammadans.—The Muhammadans came into Bengal in 1203 A.D., and since then their number commenced to increase. They consist of the descendants of the old Afghan and Mughal conquerors of Bengal and of converts from low Hindu, aboriginal and Arakanese tribes. The Muhammadans are divided into two well-known sects, Sunnis and Shias. The Sunni Muhammadans are also divided into several classes, according to their descent. The four principal of these are the following :— Sayyid, claiming descent from Ali, the son-in-law of Muhammad; Shaikh, claiming descent from the Khalifas Abubakr, Oman, and Othman; Mirza, or those of Mughal extraction; and Khan or Pathan, those claiming Afghan descent.

Religious Division of the People.—The population of Bengal, at the present time, consists of Hindus, Muhammadans, Brahma-Samaj followers, Christians, Jains and Buddhists. The *Hindus* are the most numerous

ANCIENT KINGDOMS.

section of the community. There are two sects of Hindus, who differ considerably from their fellow Hindus, in as much as they professedly abjure caste. They are the *Chaitanya Sampradáya Vaishnavs* and the *Kartábhajás*. The *Muhammadans* though divided into two sects, and subdivided into different trades and professions, are not recognised as distinct castes. They eat and drink together and intermarry. The *Christians* include Europeans, Americans, Eurasians, Native-Christians, &c. The *Brahma-Samaj* followers have been recruited since the year 1829, when Raja Ram Mohan Rai established the Brahma Samaj in Calcutta. The *Jain* religion is followed by the Marwaris. The *Buddhist* population consists of the Maghs, Chinese and Nepalese. The remainder of the population consists of hill tribes professing aboriginal faiths. Large numbers of these have now adopted other religions.

CHAPTER IV.

ANCIENT KINGDOMS OF BENGAL.

Early history.—No written history of Bengal has come down to us. Its early history is therefore obscure.

Important Ancient Kingdoms.—In ancient times Bengal was divided into a number of independent kingdoms, each governed by its own princes. The most important of them were *Magadha, Vriji, Champa, Tripura, Tamralipta, Malla-Bhumi, Birbhum, Kamrup, Odra,* and *Banga*.

Magadha.—Both in the Ramayan and the Mahabharat, the name of Magadha or modern Behar is mentioned. Its king was Jarasandha whose capital city was Giribraja, which was in or near the present town Rajagriha or Rajgir in the district of Patna. When Gautama, the founder of the Buddhist religion flourished, Ajata Satru was the king of Magadha. He built the city of Pataliputra or Kusumapura. According to the Buddhist accounts, when Buddha crossed the Ganges on his last journey from Rajagriha to Vaisali, the two ministers of Ajata Satru were engaged in building a fort at the village of Patali, as a check upon the ravages of Vriji. It was finished in the time of Udaya about 450 B.C. This Pataliputra is identified with the present city of Patna. According to the Hindu chronologies, Udaya was the thirty-seventh king of Magadha, dating from Sahadeva who was contemporary with the great war of the Mahabharat. The thirteenth in succession from Udaya was Chandra Gupta who was reigning at Pataliputra when Megasthenes came as ambassador from Seleucus Nicator, the successor of Alexander the Great, about the year 300 B. C. From his writings we can know many things existing at the time in this country. The next account that we have of Patna is supplied by Hiouen Thsang, the Chinese pilgrim who entered the city after his return from Nepal about the 20th February, 637 A. D. At that time, the kingdom of Magadha was subject to Harsha Varddhana, the great king of Kanauj. Since then Patali seems to have slowly fallen into a state of decay; and in 1266 A.D. it was little better than a nest of robbers, who had to be punished by the Mughal Government.

Vriji.—The people of Vriji were called Wajjians. The kingdom was adjoining to Pataliputra. It formed part of the great kingdom of Magadha, which extended south of the Ganges from Benares to Hiranya Parvata or Monghyr, and southwards as far as Kirana Suvarna or Singhbhum. We know nothing more of Vriji and so also of many other principalities into which Magadha was divided. Magadha, however, attained at one time to its highest glory and became the central seat of Buddhism, during the reign of Asoka, the grandson of Chandra Gupta. Asoka made it the state religion. He supported 64,000 Buddhist priests.

Champa.—Another principality of the Magadha kingdom was known as Champa. It was the kingdom of the Karna Rajas and their fort was named Karnagarh. The people in the vicinity pretend, that this Karna was the half brother of Yudhisthira by the mother's side. Probably he was a different Karna. Some consider that the kingdom of Champa coincides with the present district of Bhagalpur, others consider it to be the same with Anga, or the western part of Birbhum. Perhaps the kingdom of Karna may have included both territories. The princes of Champa, were of the Jain religion, as Vasupujya, the twelfth great teacher of that school was born at their capital, and many monuments of that religion are in the vicinity. Near Bhagalpur is Champanagar where there is the mausoleum of a Muhammadan saint. It contains places of worship of the religion which prevailed during the government of the Karna Rajas. It is related that here the husband of Behula died, stung by a serpant; but she restored him to life in virtue of her faithfulness.

Even at the present day a fair is held here in her honor.

Tripura.—Another kingdom was Kamalanka or Kamilla or Tripura. The name Tripura, now corrupted to Tipperah, was probably given to the country, in honor of the goddess *Tripuresvari* the mistress of the three worlds. The remains of the temple of the goddess still exist at Udaipur the old capital. The Rajas of Tripura claim their descent from Drujha son of Jajati. Trilochan was the king whose name is mentioned in the Mahabharat. It is impossible to define the limits of the ancient kingdom of Tipperah, but when it rose to its highest power, its conquests extended from the Sunderbans in the west to Arakan in the east and from Kamrup in the north to Arakan in the south. The military fame of the Tripura Rajas rose to its greatest height during the sixteenth century when Raja Sri Dhyan invaded with success the countries to the north, east, south and west of Tripura. The present semi-independent Raja of Hill Tipperah is a descendant of this line of kings.

Tamralipta.—In ancient times Tamralipta was a famous city and is mentioned in the sacred writings of the Hindus. It was the Sanskrit name of Tamluk, and was a Bhuddhist maritime port. From here the Chinese pilgrim Fa Hian took shipping to Ceylon in the early part of the fifth century. Numerous wealthy merchants and ship-owners resided here and carried on an extensive over-sea trade. In 635 A. D. the Chinese traveller Hiouen Thsang found the city washed away by the ocean. It has since been reformed and the sea is now fully sixty miles distant. The earliest kings of Tamluk belonged to the Peacock dynasty and were Kshattriya by caste. The last of this line Nisankha Narayan died childless. At his death the throne was usurped by a powerful aboriginal chief named Kalu Bhuiya who was the founder of the line of Kaibarta or Fisher-kings of Tamluk. They were the descendants of aboriginal Bhuiyas who embraced Hinduism. There can still be seen at Tamluk a very old temple sacred to the goddess Barga-Bhima or Kali, situated on the bank of the Rupnarayan. Many old religious stories are told regarding the sanctity of the place.

Legendary Stories.—An ancient legend relates that King Yudhisthir once resolved to perform the great *aswamedha jajna* or horse sacrifice. Arjun was in command of the horse, with a large army. When the army arrived at Tamluk, Tamradhwaj a monarch of the Peacock dynasty, seized the horse, defeated Arjun and his army and took him and Krishna prisoners. He carried them in triumph to the town but his father reproved him for daring to take Krishna who was Vishnu himself. In order to retain Krishna and Arjun always with him, the king built a great temple and placed their images within it. These images were called Jishnu and Narayan,—the former meaning 'the victorious' is Arjun and the latter Krishna. Another Hindu legend is told about the sanctity of the place. When Mahadeva destroyed Daksha and cut his head, the severed head fixed in his hand, as Daksha was a Brahman. He visited all the sacred places but was unable to release himself. He then performed austerities in the Himalayas as a penance for his sin. Vishnu appeared to him and told him to visit Tamralipta. He did so, bathed in a pool between the temples of Barga-Bhima and Jishnu-Narayan and Daksha's head fell from his hand. This place was hence called *Kapal Mochan* or the 'Release of the Head.' In course of time the rivers washed away the site. Pilgrims still bathe in the river where the old Vishnuvite temple formerly stood.

Malla-Bhumi.—Malla-Bhumi was the most ancient and most important kingdom of Bengal. It is now included in the districts of Bardwan, Bankura, and Birbhum. The family of the Raja of Bishnupur reigned here. Traditional account says that the founder of the dynasty was Raghunath Sing who derived his origin from the king of Jainagar near Brindaban. The Raja of Jainagar set out for Purushottam and passed through Bishnupur. In the forest his wife gave birth to a son whom the parents left in the woods and proceeded on their journey. A woodman named Sri Kasmetia an aboriginal Bagdi took the infant home and reared him. When the child reached the age of seven, a Brahman struck with his beauty and signs of royalty, took him to his house. The boy used to tend his cattle. One day, a cow belonging to Raghu's herd strayed and the boy, going in search of her entered a thick forest and looked in all directions but could not find her. Overcome with fatigue he lay down at the foot of a tree and fell asleep. A huge cobra glided to the place and shaded his face from the rays of the sun by erecting its hood. The Brahman, missing the boy, went out in search of him and to his horror found the deadly snake, with hood erect, as if to strike him. When he approached, the snake contracted its hood and glided away and the boy started up. One day the boy found a golden brick in a water-course. The Brahman from all these understood that the child would in future be a great man. Soon after the aboriginal king of the place having died, his funeral feast was celebrated with pomp. The Brahman taking the boy Raghu with him, went to enjoy the feast. When the Brahman was in the middle of his repast the late king's elephant seized Raghu with his trunk and approached the empty throne and carefully placed the lad on it. The multitude took this act of the elephant to be the will of God and crowned the boy on the spot. Raghunath Sing therefore was the first Aryan king of Bishnupur. He is known in history as the king of the Bagdis. He was the first of a race who reigned in Bishnupur nearly 1100 years. The kingdom is also called Jungle Mahals or forest country. The city of Bishnupur was strongly fortified, the remains of which still exist. The old Rajas dug many tanks, built many temples, encouraged trade and improved the fortifications. Even by the Muhammadan Nawabs their power was acknowledged. They were formally exempted from personal attendance at the court of Murshidabad and appeared by a representative at the Durbar.

Birbhum.—Birbhum is known as a place of heroes and Bagdis. They wore long hair and silver *balas*. For arms they had spears and javelins. Bir Sing was the first Hindu king of Birbhum and Nagar or Rajnagar was his capital. It was a place of considerable consequence and note. Many kings and Zamindars owned his power. The ruins of palaces, forts and tanks are still to be seen in Birsingpur, six miles west of the present Suri. After Birsing's death the throne passed into the hands of the Pathan princes.

There were other kings who reigned in other parts of Birbhum. During the reign of the Vaidya family, the kings of Birbhum were Lausen, Ichhai Ghosh, Shangai, Gidhor and Mallar Sing. But we know little more than their names. There is still a forest visible on the banks of the river Ajai called Senpahari. It contains a temple called Ichhai Mandir and a fort called Shyam Rup Garh said to be built by Ichhai Ghosh. He was overpowered by king Lausen. The event is chronicled in *Dharmamangal* by Ghanaram.

Kamrup.—Kamrup was the ancient kingdom which comprised Rangpur, Assam, Manipur, Jayantiya, Cachar and parts of Maimansing and Sylhet. Bhagadatta was its Raja who in the war of the Mahabharat espoused the side of Durjyadhan and was slain by Arjun. According to *Ain-i Akbari*, Bhagadatta had twenty-three successors in his dynasty and the Yagini Tantra gives some very misty accounts of the subsequent kings. Of the earliest kings of the dynasty there are traces of only one Prithu Raja. The ruins of his city lie in the present district of Jalpaiguri.

The next dynasty was that of the Pals whose first king was Bhupal or Lokpal. Those of his successors whose names are known to us were Dharma Pal, Gopi Pal, Deb Pal, and Mohi Pal. The last has immortalized his name by digging a large tank called *Mahipal dighi*. It is situated in the district of Dinagepur. An amusing story is told about the decline of the Pal dynasty. The last but one of the Pal Rajas was Bhaba Chandra. He was called Udai Chandra whence the name of his city Udaipur, now filled with impenetrable jungle. The Raja was a favourite of his goddess, whom he could visit at any time except on some forbidden days. But the Raja by mistake visited the goddess on the forbidden day and offended her. By the curse of his goddess he and his minister lost their common sense. His minister was named Gaba Chandra. Since then they committed mistakes in every thing and did nothing like other men. They slept by day and remained awake throughout the night. Some merchants lost their vessels in a storm and the Raja and his minister ordered that the potters should compensate them, for by the smoke they caused clouds, the clouds caused storm and the storm damaged the vessels. Two travellers were found one day digging the ground for a cooking place, by the side of a tank. The Raja who discovered them at once concluded that they were digging a hole to steal the tank, and he sentenced them to be impaled as robbers. The two travellers in the time of danger played a trick. Each of them expressed a wish to be impaled on the taller of the two poles. When the Raja asked them the reason, they explained that whoever was impaled on the taller pole, would in the next birth become the lord of the whole world, while the other would be his minister. Bhaba Chandra thought that such low men should not acquire such supreme dignity and so impaled himself on the taller pole. His faithful minister followed his master and expired on the shorter pole. Bhaba Chandra's successor was the last of the line. The story clearly proves that a state of anarchy followed during the reigns of the last kings. The Koch, Mech, Gáro, Bhot, Lepchá, and and other wild tribes then overran Kamrup.

The next dynasty had three Rajas.—Niladhwaj, Chakradhwaj and Nilambar. The first founded Kamatapur the ruins of which are situated in the Kuch Behar territory on the eastern part of the Dharla river. Nilambar attained to great power. His dominions included the greater part of Kamrup, the whole, of Rangpur as far as Goraghat to the south, where he built a fort. He laid out a magnificent road from Kamatapur to Goraghat much of which is still in good preservation. It forms part of the main road between Kuch Behar, Rangpur and Bogra. He was by the treachery of his minister taken prisoner by the Afghans.

Next came the Koch to the front and uniting under Hajo founded the Koch or Kuch Behar dynasty, which exists to the present day.

Odra or Utkala.—They are the ancient names of the kindom of the Uriya-speaking people. Odra is the original name, while Utkala is its Sanskrit name. Perhaps Orissa is the corruption of *Odra-desa*. Its early history is obtained from the palm-leaf records, that is accounts written over on palm-leaves with a sharp iron pen without ink. It gives a list of 107 kings of Orissa with exact dates for their reigns, from 3101 B. C., down to the present day. During the first three thousand years or up to 57 B.C. twelve kings are said to have reigned in Orissa, each reigning on an average a little more than 250 years. The reign of the first king, Sankar Deva, is assigned from 1807 to 1407 B. C. During the reign of his successor Gautama Deva, the Aryans pushed their way down to the Godavari river. These Sanskrit-speaking colonists marched down the valley of the Ganges and skirting round Bengal, reached Orissa. About 500 years before the Christian era, the palm-leaf record says, the Yavanas invaded Orissa under one Rakta-Bahu. It has been concluded that these Yavans were the Greeks or Græco-Bactrians.

The period of the Yavana inroads into Orissa is contemporary with the establishment of Buddhism in the province. This was the period, during which the Buddhists honey-combed the mountains and excavated the rock monasteries of Orissa. This was the period of defeat and degradation to the Brahmanical faith.

The expulsion of the Yavana dynasty from Orissa was completed in 474 A. D. and the restoration of the Brahmanical faith commenced. Yayati Kesari was the Raja who expelled the Yavanas and was the founder of the Kesari or Lion dynasty. After a struggle of 150 years beween Bhuddhism and Brahmanism the latter again established its supremacy. The founder of the Lion dynasty sought out the image of Jagannath in the jungles where it lay hidden during the Yavana occupation and brought it back to Puri in triumph. He commenced the construction of the great temple at Bhuvanesvar. The earlier kings of the Lion dynasty held their court sometimes at Bhuvanesvar the city of Temples dedicated to Siva in the Puri district and sometimes at Jajpur situated on the Baitarini river. A king of this dynasty named Nripa Kesari who reigned between 941 and 953 A. D. founded the city of Cuttack, still the capital of Orissa. His son Makar Kesari constructed the masonry embankment of the Mahanadi river, several miles long, by blocks of hewn stones to protect the city from inundation. This embankment exists to the present time. Madhav Kesari was the Raja who strengthened the capital by building the fortress of Sarangarh between 971 and 989 A. D. About 500 years after Matsya Kesari built the massive bridge by which the pilgrims enter Puri at this day. The dynasty came to an end with Subarna Kesari who died childless in 1132 A.D. and was succeeded by Chor-ganga who invaded the kingdom and conquered it.

The family name of the new dynasty was *Ganga-vansa* or Gangetic line. Chor-ganga appears from an inscription to have carried his arms into the Western Districts of Bengal and to have sacked Bardhaman identified as the city of Bardwan. His son Gangeswar carried his conquest far and wide. His territory reached from the Godavari to the Gangetic valley and embraced the whole eastern coast of India. Ananga Bhim Deo the fifth monarch of the dynasty, who reigned between 1175 and 1202, built the present temple of Jagannath. Protap Rudra Deva was the last king of the Gangetic line who reigned from 1504 to 1532 A. D. The king in his early years leaned to the Buddhist creed but was converted by the great Vishnuvite reformer Chaitanya who visited Puri at this time. He left 32 sons two of whom succeeded him for about a year a-piece. The prime minister sooner or later murdered every male member of the family and himself seized the kingdom 1534 A. D. About 24 years after, the fierce Muhammadan general Kala Pahar, swept like a wave across the Province, threw down the temples, smashed the idols, drove Jagannath himself into hiding and exterminated the last of the independent dynasties of Orissa.

Banga-desa or Bengal Proper.—There is a tradition, that in the east of Bengal the celebrated Hindu Raja Bikramaditya held his court for some years. He gave his name to the Parganah of Bikrampur. The next rulers spoken of were the Bhuiya or Buddhist Rajas, who were of the Pal-dynasty-kings of Bengal. Three of them took up their abode to the north of the Buriganga and Dhaleswari, where the sites of their capital are still to be seen. Jas Pal resided at Madhavpur in Talipabad; Haris Chandra at Katibari, near Sabhar; and Sisu Pal at Kapasia in Bhawal, in the district of Dacca. The dynasty of Adisur is supposed to have reigned, at the same time, in the tract lying south of the Buriganga river. He was the founder of the Sen family and he was otherwise called Bir Sen. He reigned in the beginning of the eleventh century. In the year 1063 A. D. Adisur, finding the Brahmans of the country unfit to act in the ceremonies which his wife intended to be performed, sent to the king of Kanauj in Oudh for some learned Brahmans. The following five Brahmans of different families were despatched according to his request—namely, Daksha of the *Kasyap* family; Chhandar of the *Bátsya* family; Sriharsha of the *Bharodwdj* family; Bed Garbha of the *Sábarna* family; and Bhatta Narayan of the *Sándilya* family. Some accounts state that these Brahmans first settled in Bikrampur near Dacca, and their descendants emigrated to other districts; while others assert that they originally settled in Nadiya, and emigrated thence to Bikrampur and elsewhere. These five learned men came each attended by a servant, who called themselves Kayasthas. These five Brahmans and

Kayasthas were the ancestors of the present high classes of those castes. Adisur was succeeded by his son Ballal Sen, who is fabled to have been the son of the Brahmaputra river. He ascended the throne in 1066 A. D. In the twelfth century, there reigned a descendant of this family, who too was named Ballal Sen. Ballal Sen II. was the son of Vijoy Sen and grandson of Hemanta Sen. He found society in such a state of confusion, that he set about reforming it, and divided the Brahmans, Baidyas, Kayasthas and pure Sudras into different classes. It does not appear that the Kshatriyas and Vaisyas then existed in Bengal. He also classified the descendants of the Brahmans from Kanauj, who by that time had dispersed into fifty-six villages, in different parts of the kingdom. He made *kulins* of those, who were distinguished by the nine following qualities:—purity (*áchár*), humility (*binay*), learning (*bidyá*), good reputation (*pratisthá*), sanctity acquired by pilgrimage (*tirthadarsana*), constancy (*nishthá*), good conduct (*britti*), devotion (*tapa*), and charity (*dán*). Unfortunately he made the rank of *kulins* hereditary. Few of the present *kulins* possess the noble qualities of their ancestors. The rules of *kulinism* at present only limit intermarriage among themselves. His capital was Gaur, the ruins of which still exist in the district of Maldah; and his kingdom was very extensive. At this time Bengal was divided into five provinces. They were—(1) *Rárha*, west of the Hugli and south of the Ganges; (2) *Bágri* the Delta of the Ganges; (3) *Barendra*, the country north of the Padma and between the Karatoya and the Mahananda; (4) *Banga*, the country to the east of the delta; and (5) *Mithilá*, the country west of the Mahananda. According to these divisions also, the Brahmans and Kayasthas have acquired their distinctive names. Ballal Sen II. was an author himself. His work is entitled *Dán Ságár*. He was succeeded in 1108 A. D., by his son Lakshman Sen, who beautified the city of Gaur. The most ancient name for the city seems to have been Lakshmanawati, which is usually corrupted into Laknauti. The name of Gaur, however, is of great antiquity; and it is highly probable, that the name was applied more to the kingdom than to the city, for the Bengali language is sometimes called *Gauriya Bhasa*.

Nadiya was founded in the twelfth century by Lakshman Sen, on the banks of the Bhagirati. Ballal Sen II. and the members of his family were wont to pay frequent visits to Nadiya, for clearing their sins by washing themselves in the waters of the Bhagirati. On the other side of the river, there is still a large mould called after Ballal Sen. There is a *dighi* called *Ballali dighi*. Nadiya continued the Hindu capital till A. D. 1203. Lakshmaniya, the son of Lakshman, was the last Sen Raja of Bengal. He ruled nominally for 80 years. He was called by the Hindus Su Sen or Sura Sen.

CHAPTER V.

THE MUHAMMADAN CONQUEST OF BENGAL.

The Muhammadans.—While the Hindu kings were reigning in Bengal, and in other provinces of Hindusthan, far to the west of the river Indus, there reigned kings, whom the Hindus called *Yavans*. They were Muhammadans or the followers of the religion of Mahomed. They were barbarous and cruel, and hated the Hindus. The Hindus considered them impure, and believed that their very touch would defile them. At this time the Hindu kings had no unity, and would not unite against a foreign invasion.

Sultan Mahmud.—During the year 1000 A. D., the great Sultan of Ghazni named Mahmud came with a large army to Hindusthan. He plundered the country, and returned home with much spoil. Finding the Hindu kings weak, he came into the country twelve times, plundered it, and each time returned with vast riches. He cruelly put to death thousands of natives, broke down their temples and images of gods, and did many other acts of oppression. He however did not attempt to settle in the country.

Kutab-ud-din.—About two hundred years after, Muhammad Ghori, the king of Ghore, invaded India and utterly destroyed the old and powerful kingdoms of the Hindu kings in the North. He retained the kingdom he conquered, and making his general Kutab-ud-din governor of Delhi, returned to his country. After the death of his master, Kutab became independent, and thus became the first Muhammadan Emperor of India.

Baktiar Khiliji.—At the beginning of the thirteenth century, a valiant Afghan Muhammad Baktiar Khilji, general of Kutab-ud-din, led his followers to Behar or the kingdom of Magadh. He conquered the country and acquired great wealth by plundering it. He gave most of the riches to Kutab-ud-din, and obtained his permission to conquer Bengal. In the year 1203-4, Muhammad Baktiar Khilij led his Afghan troops under the imperial banner to Nadiya. On arriving near the city, he concealed his troops in a dense jungle, and escorted by only seventeen body guards, entered the palace. On being challanged by the Raja's *sipahis*, he informed them that he was an envoy from the Court of Delhi. He concealed his movements with such secrecy, that no suspicion arose till he and his horsemen passed the inner gates. Drawing their swords, they slaughtered the royal attendants. The Raja, who was then seated at breakfast, alarmed by the cries of his household, made his escape from the palace and fled in a small *dingi* down the river. He fled to the shrine of Jagannath, where he closed his days as an ascetic. Instead of following the fugitive king, the mass of the Muhammadan troops concealed in the forest, now advanced towards the city, and took easy possession of it. Baktiar Khilji gave the palace to be plundered by his army, and then proceeded to Laknauti or the ancient city of Gaur. He took the city without opposition. He pulled down the Hindu temples and built Muhammadan mosques on their sites. From this time, Gaur became a Muhammadan capital.

Relics of the Hindu Kingdom.—But the Bengal territory, conquered in 1203-4 by the Mahammadans, did not comprise the Eastern Districts, or the *Banga-des* proper, which remained in the possession of Ballal Sen's descendants till the end of the thirteenth century, when Sonargaon was occupied by the grandsons of the Emperor Balban.

The place, where the Hindu princes resided, is still pointed out at Rampal. There exists an enclosed space, but no traces of any building can be seen. Near it, there is a deep excavation called *Agnikunda*, where it is said the last Hindu prince of Bikrampur and his family burned themselves on the approach of the Musalmans.

Literary men of the Hindu Period.—Of the literary men, who flourished during the Hindu period, were the five Brahmans who were brought from Kanauj by Adisur. Two of them, Sri Harsa and Bhatta Narayan, wrote books. The former composed *Naisad Charita, Khandan Khanda Khádya*, and the latter the celebrated drama *Beni Sanghar*. Under the patronage of Lakshman Sen, his minister Halaudha composed his *Brahman Sarvasha*. The four poets, who were ornaments of his Court, were Umapati Dhar, Saran, Gobardhan Acharjya and Jai Dev. Jai Dev composed his *Git Gobinda* about 1200 A. D. He was a native of the village called Kendabilla or Kenduli on the river Ajai, in the District of Birbhum. There a *mela* is still held in his honor.

CHAPTER VI.

DEPENDENT PATHAN KINGS OF BENGAL.

Baktiar Khiliji (1203-1205.)—Having established himself on the throne of Gaur, Baktiar Khiliji divided his newly conquered territory into two parts. *Rárh* and *Mithilá* formed one part with its capital at Laknauti, and *Bágri* and *Barendra* the other part with its capital at Deakot. He next determined to invade Kamrup, and crossed the Brahmaputra with a large army. But he met with great disaster and was obliged to retreat, his whole army being cut off by the Raja of Kamrup. He returned to Deakot, where he died a short time after. In A. D. 1205 or two years after the conquest of Bengal, Baktiar Khiliji commenced constructing a high way from Deakot to Nagor, a distance of ten days, journey.

Ghias-ud-din (1211-1227.)—A state of anarchy followed the death of Baktiar Khiliji. His officers chose the most powerful amongst them as governor, who ruled from 1205 to 1209 A. D. The Emperor of Delhi hearing of it, sent an army which conquered the country. Ali Mardan was appointed governor, but the Khiliji chiefs murdered him and made their chief Hisam-ud-din Daud Ghias-ud-din governor in 1211 A. D. He held his court in Gaur, which he beautified with splendid buildings. He completed the road from Nagar to Deakot, commenced in the reign of Baktiar. In 1218 A. D.

he committed a raid on Orissa and forced it to pay tribute, though he failed to make a permanent conquest. He also compelled the king of Kamrup to pay him tribute. He was a wise and powerful prince, and administered justice with impartiality. He was much liked by the Emperor Altamash but unfortunately for himself he declared himself independent. The Emperor sent an army against him under the command of his second son Nasir-ud-din, who defeated him and slew him in battle 1227 A. D.

Taghan Khan (1237-1245.)—Prince Nasir-ud-din reigned for some years in Gaur where he died. Three governors were then successively sent from Delhi, of whom the last was Aza-ud-din Taghan Khan. He was appointed governor in 1237 and reigned till 1245 A. D. In A. D. 1243 he marched against Orissa, but the persistent valour of the Uriyas drove him into the heart of Bengal. He was pursued by them up to his own capital, which they besieged. In A. D. 1244 the town of Nagar was plundered by the Uriyas. Taghan Khan in his difficulty applied to the Emperor of Delhi for assistance, who sent Timur Khan the Governor of Oudh to his aid. The Uriyas retreated on the approach of Timur, but the latter was so much pleased with Bengal that he determined to keep it himself. A battle ensued between the two Muhammadan chiefs and Taghan was defeated. He was allowed to retire with all his property; and soon after he was appointed Governor of Oudh. Timur reigned two years.

Taghral Khan (1246-1258.)—Taghral Khan was appointed governor in 1246 A. D. His first act was to march against the King of Orissa to take vengeance on him. This invasion of Orissa by the Muhammadans, attempted ten years later, also failed completely. Taghral was defeated and obliged to return with disgrace. He then invaded Sribatta (Sylhet) and obtained much plunder. He next marched against Kamrup. Though at first victory leaned to his side, ultimately he was completely defeated, taken prisoner and put to death A. D. 1258.

Maghis-ud-din Taghral (1277-1282.)—Within the space of next nineteen years, three governors of no great note reigned. In A. D. 1277 Maghis-ud-din Taghral was appointed governor. At this time, Ratnafah, a brother of the king of Tipperah, had been residing for some years in Gaur, beseeching the assistance of the king of Gaur, to invade the kingdom of Tipperah and usurp the throne of his brother. About A. D. 1279, the king of Gaur helped the prince by invading the territory of Tipperah and conquering it for him. He also conferred on him the title of *Manik* (a pearl) which the Rajas of Tipperah have ever since retained. By this invasion, the king of Gaur obtained immense wealth, and a large number of elephants. Elated with it, and hearing that Emperor Balban had grown old and weak, he declared himself independent. When the emperor heard of it, he sent two armies one after the other, to subdue the rebel, but both were defeated. Enraged at this, the Emperor collected a large army and marched in person against the governor of Bengal, and crushed the revolt with merciless skill. Taghral fled, on the approach of the Emperor, towards Tipperah with all his wealth and troops. The Emperor pursued him. The imperial general Muhammad Sher got information of the whereabouts of the fugitive, and with only forty horsemen darted into the rebel camp, shouting out 'victory to the great Emperor Balban', and put every one he met to the sword. Taghral himself jumped on a horse and fled towards the river. Muhammed Sher followed him close, seized him while he attempted to cross the river, and cut off his head. The Emperor returned to Gaur with much plunder, and mercilessly butchered all who sided with the rebel governor, together with their wives and children. In A. D. 1282 he made his own son Governor of Bengal, under the title of Nasir-ud-din.

Nasir-ud-din (1282–1292.)—While Nasir-ud-din was reigning in Bengal, his elder brother died, and he became the heir-apparent to the great throne of Delhi. But he preferred his quiet life in Bengal. Accordingly his son Kaikobad became the Emperor of Delhi, when the old Emperor died. Kaikobad was licentious and addicted to pleasure. Nasir-ud-din therefore wrote a letter to his son, to give up luxury and attend to business, but to no avail. He therefore marched to Delhi with an army against his son, and the son advanced to meet him. The two armies encamped in sight of each other in the plains of Behar The old king wrote a letter to have an interview with his son. Kaikobad agreed, but at the advice of his wicked minister Nizam-ud-din, he proposed that in order to maintain his dignity as Emperor of Delhi, his father should prostrate himself before him three times. The time of meeting arrived, and as the old man entered the presence of his son, he prostrated himself to the ground. He made a second prostration and when he was about to make a third, his son, unable to bear the sight, left the throne, embraced his father, and implored forgiveness. A reconciliation took place, and Nasir-ud-din remaining with his son for some days and giving him good advice, returned to his own country, where he reigned peacefully till his death A. D. 1292.

No sooner Kaikobad returned to Delhi than he resigned himself to his old habits, and was soon after assassinated in A.D. 1290 by Jalal-ud-din, the first Emperor of the Khiliji dynasty.

East Bengal conquered by the Muhammadans.— The two sons of Nasir-ud-din, named Kai Kaus and Firoz Shah, successively reigned in Gaur after him. Firoz Shah died in 1317-18, and his eldest son Shihab-ud-din ascended the throne of Laknauti. His brother Bahadur Shah, to make a kingdom of his own, attacked the country of Eastern Bengal, where the descendants of Ballal Sen were then reigning. Tradition relates, that the Hindu prince fought bravely and defeated the invader of his territory. But an unfortunate accident happened, which closed the Hindu dynasty. When the Prince went out to meet the enemy, he carried with him a messenger-pigeon, leaving instructions to his family, that if the bird returned, it should be regarded as the signal of defeat, and the whole family should put themselves to death. Though the Prince gained the victory, the bird escaped from his garment in which it was concealed, and flew to its destination. The Raja hurried home, but it was too late. When he reached, he found all the family burnt in the *Agnikunda* (see p. 42) still smoking with their ashes, and he also cast himself upon the funeral pile and perished.

Bahadur Shah occupied the kingdom and made Sonargaon including Dacca his capital.

After a time Bahadur Shah became very tyrannical, and expelled his brother Shihab-ud-din from the throne of Laknauti. Shihab-ud-din sought the aid of the Emperor Ghias-ud-din Tughluk, who at this time occupied the imperial throne of Delhi, by driving out the Khiliji dynasty. The Emperor Ghias-ud-din marched to Bengal and leaving Nassir-ud-din, the brother of Shihab-ud-din, as king of Laknauti, carried off Bahadur Shah as a prisoner to Delhi.

In A. D. 1325 Muhammad Tughluk ascended the throne of Delhi, and reinstated Bahadur Shah as king of Bengal. Bahadur, however, did not long remain submissive to the Emperor of Delhi. He declared himself independent, and struck coin in his own name. In A. D. 1330 Muhammad Tughlak marched into Bengal, defeated Bahadur and slew him. Having conquered Eastern Bengal, he divided the country into three Provinces—Laknauti, Satgaon and Sonargaon, in A. D. 1331. He left Tatar Bahram as Governor of Sonargaon including Dacca, the capital of East Bengal; and appointed Kadar Khan Governor of Laknauti, the capital of West Bengal ; and Azam-ul-mulak Governor of Satgaon or Saptagram, the capital of South Bengal.

CHAPTER VII.

INDEPENDENT PATHAN KINGS OF BENGAL.

Shams-ud-din (1339—1358.)—No sooner Muhammad Tughluk returned to Delhi, than the state again fell into disorder. On the death of Bahram Khan in A. D. 1338, his armour bearer Fakhr-ud-din seized the government of Sonargaon and reigned for more than ten years under the title of Mubarak Shah. After his death, his son Mujafar Gazi Shah became Governor of East Bengal. In Western Bengal, Ali-ud-din Ali Shah established his independence and transferred the seat of government to Panduah, beyond the Mahananda. In order to decorate the new city with buildings, all the public monuments that could be removed, were taken from Gaur. Hence it is that in the ruins of Panduah we still find stones bearing Hindu sculptures. Shams-ud-din Ilias Khwajah set up a rival claim against Ali Shah in 1339. After a long and protracted war, Ali Shah was defeated and killed. In 1345 Shams-ud-din became master of Panduah, whose court-name was Firozabad. From this time the name of Firozabad appeared in coins, and the name of Laknauti (Gaur) disappeared. In 1351 Shams-ud-din occupied East Bengal, though the son and son-in-law of Mubarak Shah attempted to retain possession of it. Hence the whole of Bengal was united again, and Sonargaon became the residence of governors, generally sons of the reigning king.

Ilias Shah or Shams-ud-in next extended his dominion in the north-west as far as Benares, and marched against the Imperial Governor of Behar. The emperor Firoz III., in order to punish him, came down with an army. Ilias Shah left his son to defend Panduah, and himself fled and took refuge in the fort of Ekdala 11 miles distant. Panduah was easily taken, and Ekdala was besieged by the emperor's army. The emperor failed to take the fort and was obliged to give up the siege. He was satisfied with presents from Ilias Shah and acknowledged his independence, and fixed the limits of his kingdom up to the river Gandak A. D. 1357. Haji Ilias Shah, as Shams-ud-in was called, then founded the town of Hajipore on its bank opposite to Patna. There he built a stone mosque known by the name of *Juma Masjid*. He built also the famous fort covering an area of 360 bighas, of which the ramparts are still visible. He reigned in Bengal for 19 years and died in 1358 A. D.

Sekandar Shah (1358—1389.)—The eldest son of Shams-ud-in succeeded him under the title of Sekandar Shah. No sooner the emperor heard that Ilias was dead, than he raised an army and again attacked Bengal. Following his father, Sekandar Shah took refuge in the fort of Ekdala, which he most successfully defended. In A. D. 1359, finding it difficult to gain the fort, the emperor returned to Delhi after receiving a present of elephants from the king. In A. D. 1361 Sekandar erected the famous mosque called Adina mosque in Panduah, the ruins of which may still be seen. Sekandar had two wives; by one he had sixteen sons, and by the other one named Azam Shah. The latter, finding that his step mother was contriving means to murder him, revolted and for some time reigned in East Bengal independently. Here he invited the poet Hafiz of Persia to his court but Hafiz declined the invitation for fear of taking such a long journey. Sekandar marched with an army to meet him; a battle ensued and he was killed.

Ghias-ud-din (1389—1398.)—Azam Shah ascended the throne of Bengal under the title of Ghias-ud-in. His first cruel act was to put out the eyes of his half-brothers, which he did for his self-preservation. He however ruled Bengal for nine years with justice and moderation. He died in A. D. 1398. Some say, he was murdered by a powerful Hindu Raja named Ganes, who was called Raja Kans by the Muhammadans. Others say, that Ghias-ud-in was succeeded by his son and grandson, and Ganes after killing the latter seated himself on the throne.

Raja Kans and his Successors (1405—1445.)— Raja Ganes, his son and grand-son reigned in Bengal for forty years. But at this time the power of Bengal was weakened. East Bengal fell a prey to the Rajas of Tipperah, Kamrup and Arakan. Ibrahim the great Sultan of Joanpur encroached on the western frontier of Bengal, and added the whole of Behar to his kingdom. Ganes ruled with impartiality and was liked both by the Hindus and Muhammadans. When he died, the Muhammadans demanded his body for burial, and the Hindus claimed it for cremation. He built many Hindu temples at Panduah. His son Jadu succeeded him. He converted himself to Muhammadanism and took the name of Jelal-ud-din Muhammed Shah. He transferred the court from Panduah to Gaur and adorned it with magnificent buildings. After his death, his son Ahmad Shah succeeded him. He was very oppressive, and was assassinated by two of his slaves in the year 1445 A. D.

Nazir Shah and his Successors (1445—1487.)— The Muhammadan nobles then raised Nazir Shah a descendant of Ilias Shah to the throne, who reigned peacefully for thirty-one years. He strongly fortified Gaur and erected its splendid gates. He was succeeded by his son Barbek Shah, who first introduced Abyssinian and negro slaves into his court. He was succeeded by his son who ruled seven years. The latter died without issue, and so the nobles raised Fatteh Shah a younger son of Nazir, to the throne. The Abyssinians or *Habsis* became very powerful now, and the king in going to restrain their power was put to death.

Abyssinian Governors (1487—1494.)—The chief eunuch then became king, and assumed the name of Sultan Shah Zada. In eight months he was in his turn assassinated by Malik Indil his Abyssinian General-in-chief. Both he and his son reigned for four years. Muzaffar Shah succeeded the latter. He was a great tyrant and the people grew tired of him. His Vizir Husain Shah rebelled and besieged him in his capital. The king came out and gave him battle. More than twenty thousand men were slain in the field of battle before Gaur, among whom was the king himself A. D. 1494.

Husain Shah (1494—1523.)—The throne of Bengal was now occupied by Husain Shah. He was one of the powerful rulers of Bengal. He was connected with the family of the prophet Muhammad. When he came to Bengal he was in an humble situation. By dint of his ability he became prime minister, and at last king of Bengal. On ascending the throne, his first act was to reform the government, which was in a state of great disorder, on account of the anarchy that prevailed in the reign of the previous rulers. He at once hit that the Abyssinian slaves and eunuchs and the *Paiks* were the cause of all disorders. He expelled the former, who now proceeded to the Deccan, where they became famous under the name of *Sidhis*. The latter he removed to the frontiers of Orissa, by giving them small pieces of *Jaigir* lands to protect him in the time of invasion.

At this time Sochi Patra, the prime minister of Raja Nilambhar of Kamatapur, came to the court of Gaur to procure an invasion of the country of his master, in order to take vengeance for the wrongs done to him (see p. 34). The Muhammadan commander failed to take the place and proposed peace. He asked and obtained permission for Musalman ladies to go and pay their respects to the Hindu queen, but in the litters armed men were concealed who captured the town. Nilambhar was taken prisoner and put into an iron cage to be carried to Gaur, but he escaped from the way. A disastrous expedition was next made into Assam, which slackened the hold of the Mahammadans on the dominion they occupied in Rangpur. The limit of their possessions northward, was now fixed by an irregular line drawn from the Karatoya on the west crossing the Ghaghat and Tista midway, extending to the Brahmaputra on the east. The succeeding Koch dynasty afterwards built a line of fortifications all along this boundary, which is still in excellent preservation.

In about A. D. 1510, Husain Shah sent his general Ismail Gazi to conquer Orissa. He dashed down upon the Province, sacked its capital Cuttack and plundered the holy city Puri. The Orissa prince, who was engaged with his rebellious vassals in the south, hurried to meet the general and succeeded to beat him back. At this time, the king of Jaunpur was defeated by the emperor of Delhi Sekandar Lodi, and he took refuge in the court of Husain Shah who received him honorably and gave him a pension. The emperor of Delhi, in pursuing the king of Jaunpur, came to the confines of Bengal and threatened to attack it, but a peace was concluded between him and Husain Shah. According to the terms of the treaty, Behar, Tirhut and Sarun were ceded to the emperor, provided he would not invade Bengal again. He reigned prosperously for twenty-nine years and died in A. D. 1523.

Nasrat Shah (1523—1533.)—Husain was succeeded by his son Nasrat Shah. During the early part of his reign, he showed signs of many brilliant qualities, treated his relatives and dependants with kindness, and displayed wisdom and military talents. During his reign, the Musalman possessions to the south of the northern boundary were consolidated by Ismail Gazi, the governor of Goraghat. In 1523, Nasrat Shah, better known as Nasib Shah, broke the treaty made by his father, and invaded Tirhut, and made his son-in-law Makhdum Alam governor and stationed him at Hajipur. From this time, Mungir (Monghyr) became the head-quarters of the Behar army of the Bengal kings.

INDEPENDENT PATHAN KINGS. 55

It was in this reign, that Sultan Babar came down from Cabul, and in 1526 after the battle of Panipat conquered Delhi, and established the empire of the Mughals in India. The Afghan chiefs including Muhammad Lodi, the brother of the late Sultan, took refuge in the court of Nasrat Shah. Babar marched against him, but he purchased peace by giving him costly presents. But no sooner was Babar dead than he broke the treaty, and gave all assistance he could to Ibrahim Lodi, the inveterate enemy of Babar's son Humayun. With the increase of power Nasrat Shah became tyrannical and he was assassinated in 1533 A. D. by the eunuchs of his palace, whom he treated cruelly. He erected the celebrated golden mosque called the *Sona Masjid* in Gaur.

Nasrat's son and successor Firoz Shah was murdered by his uncle Mahmud Shah, who was ultimately defeated and deposed by Sher Shah A. D. 1536.

Sher Shah (1536—1545.)—Sher Shah, a Pathan of the Sur family or tribe, was born at Sasseram in the present district of Shahabad. His original name was Farid. He was called Sher Shah for having killed a tiger in single combat, by the blow of his sword, *Sher* meaning in *Hindi* a tiger. His father held the rank of Commander of five hundred and enjoyed a *Jaigir* at Sasseram, where the ruins of his house and tomb are still pointed out. Sher Shah's life is full of adventures, but his actions were always stained with perfidy and fraud. At his early age, he left home in disgust and introduced himself to the great Babar, who, just at this time, became Emperor of Delhi. There he diligently studied the character of the Mughals and stored his mind with the knowledge, which helped him to attain his future eminence. In A. D. 1526, after Babar had established himself on the throne of Delhi, Mahmud Lohani a Pathan chief made himself master of Behar and Joanpur. Sher rose high in the estimation of Mahmud and occupied a high position in his court. At the time of the death of Mahmud, his son Prince Jalal was a minor. Sher became his Vazir, and ultimately acquired the sole power in the Province. The Lohani nobles, seeing the high power of Sher conspired to put him to death; but when the conspiracy was disclosed, Jalal fled with all his Omrahs and took refuge in the court of Mahmud Shah III., the king of Bengal.

In 1531 Sher Khan obtained possession of the strong fortress of Chunar in the province of Benares, by marrying the widow of the Afghan officer who held it. In 1533 he gained a great success in the struggles with Kutab Khan a general of high repute, who for a considerable time was in command of the army of Bengal kings located at Monghyr, the head-quarters in Behar. In 1536 he attacked Gaur. The king Mahmud Shah sought the assistance of the Portuguese General, and he sent a fleet of nine ships to his aid. But on the approach of Sher, Mahmud Shah first shut himself up in Gaur, and soon after fled and took the protection of Emperor Humayun. Gaur opened its gates and Sher Khan became the master of Bengal.

Humayun marched against Sher who was obliged to retire to Sasseram. At this time Sher managed to obtain possession of the strong fort of Rohtas. Rohtasgarh was named after Prince Rohitaswa, son of Harischandra, a king of the solar race, whose image was worshipped on the spot till destroyed by Aurangzeeb. Nothing is known as to who held the fort after Harischandra till A. D. 1100, when it was supposed to belong to Pratap Dhawala, father of the last Hindu king. Sher Khan captured Rohtasghar in 1539, and immediately began to strengthen the fortifications. But when the work had slightly progressed, he selected a more favourable site in the neighbourhood at Shergarh, which bears his name.

While Sher Khan was thus engaged in strengthening himself, Humayun was occupied at Gaur in rioting. Sher now retired westward, seized Benares and arrested the return of Humayun by occupying the passes of Bengal. It became necessary for Humayun also to return to Delhi, as one of his brothers had proclaimed himself Emperor of Agra.

On his way back to Delhi, Humayun was met by the army of Sher Khan at Chausa a village situated four miles west of Baxar, close to the east bank of the Karmanasa. For three months the imperial army lay idle in the camp, not able either to advance or fall back. At length Humayun proposed that if Sher would let him pass, he would give up Bengal and Behar to him. Sher agreed, and touching the Koran swore that he would allow the Mughal army to pass uninjured. That very night, the 26th June 1539, while the Mughal army was quite unprepared, Sher made a sudden attack on them and killed a large member of them. The rest escaped with great difficulty. Hamayun had only time to plunge into the Ganges on horseback; and it would have fared hard with him but for the friendly assistance of a water-carrier, on whose *massak* or water-bag the Emperor was supported till he reached the opposite side. The water-carrier was afterwards rewarded by being permitted to sit for half a day on the throne, with absolute power. Sher now assumed the title of Shah, and marching to Gaur proclaimed himself King of Bengal and Behar. After spending a year to consolidate the government, he marched with fifty thousand Afghans to attack the Emperor. A battle was fought near Kanauj; Humayun was defeated and fled to Persia. Sher Shah became Emperor of Delhi A. D. 1540. Sher Shah now became undisputed master of the empire, and his history now properly belongs to the Indian empire. He once more returned to Bengal to quell an insurrection. He divided Bengal into provinces, over each of which he placed a governor. During his reign Bengal enjoyed peace and prosperity. Justice was inviolate, general security reigned, and his death at the end of five years was considered a national calamity. He made a high road from Sonargaon in East Bengal to Indus, a distance of about two thousand miles, bordered with fruit trees, with wells and carvan-saries at the distance of every *kros* for the convenience of travellers. He ordered that at every stage, all travellers without distinction of race or creed should be entertained at the public expense. He was the first to introduce mounted post in India. In A. D. 1545 he was killed by the bursting of a shell, while engaged in a siege.

Muhammad Khan Sur (1545—1555.)—From A. D. 1545 to A. D. 1556 for 11 years the sons and descendants of Sher Shah reigned as Emperors of Hindusthan. His son Islam Shah appointed one of his own relatives Muhammad Khan Sur, his deputy in Bengal. He remained faithful to his master and benefactor, but as soon as Muhammad Adil Shah became Emperor of Delhi, he declared himself independent and made conquests in the province of Joanpur. In the following year, Adil Shah sent his Hindu General Himu against him, who defeated and killed him A. D. 1555.

Bahadur Shah (1555—1561.)—Muhammad Khan was succeeded by his son and successor Bahadur Shah. In A. D. 1545, we find Monghyr mentioned as in possession of Miyan Sulaiman an Afghan of the Kararani tribe, who held South Behar for Islam Shah son of Ser Shah. Sulaiman with the view of securing his independence, entered into an alliance with Bahadur Shah. When Adil Shah, or Adli as he is generally called, retired before the advancing army of Akbar, Bahadur Shah and Sulaiman attacked him near Surajgarh, west of Monghyr, and defeated and killed him A. D. 1557. This confirmed Bahadur Shah in the government of Bengal and Behar, and he reigned in those provinces peacefully till A. D. 1561.

Bahadur was succeeded by his brother Julal-ud-in who at the end of three years died at Gaur. His son a youth was then raised to the throne, but was assassinated immediately after, and an obscure man ascended the throne.

Sulaiman Kararani (1563—1572.)—Bengal was in a state of anarchy now, and Sulaiman sent his brother Taj Khan into Bengal with a powerful army. He defeated the usurper and reigned for a year in Gaur as his brother's deputy. In A. D. 1563 Taj Khan died, and Sulaiman himself proceeded to Bengal and became ruler of Bengal and Behar. He acknowleged the suzerainty of Akbar by sending him valuable presents. By this prudent measure, he secured the friendship of Akbar and ruled Bengal in peace till A. D. 1572.

The greatest event in the reign of Sulaiman was his conquest of Orissa. This invasion of Orissa was undertaken by the Muhammadans, half a century after the previous invasion by the general of Husain Shah. In 1567-68 Sulaiman advanced with a large army under his general Kala Pahar into Orissa, and defeated the last independent king of Orissa Raja Mukund Deo, under the walls of Jajpur. The Hindu prince was slain in the battle. From this time, the representatives of this line have been merely Rajas of Khurdha, and the hereditary custodians of the temple and idol of Jagannath.

Kala Pahar was by birth a Brahman, but he fell in love with a princess of Gaur and became a Musalman in order to marry her. Since then he became a violent persecutor of the Hindus, and perpetrated devastations on every Hindu temple and idol that fell in his sight. After the death of the Orissa king, he was not content like the previous invaders, with levying a ransom from the province but marched through it and besieged Puri. The veteran Afghans marched from temple to temple, throwing down the most august shrines, and smashing the idols. The wealth of Jagannath protected him from the hand of the impure Musalmans, who made a profit out of him by licensing his worship in the shape of a pilgrim tax, which was estimated to have amounted to nine lakhs of *sikka* Rupees.

In the year following the conquest, the Afghan King

took his departure from Orissa, leaving the government of the country in the hands of his deputy Khan Jahan, to whom Kutlu Khan was subordinate as Governor of Puri. No sooner he turned his back than Orissa again revolted. The Bengal king immediately marched southwards with his Afghan veterans and succeeded in restoring his supremacy. In A. D. 1564, eleven years before the final depopulation of Gaur, Sulaiman Shah moved the seat of his government to Tandan or Tangra.

Daud Khan (1572—1576.)—Sulaiman was succeeded by his son Bayazid, who was soon set aside and Daud Shah his younger brother was raised to the throne. Sulaiman Khan by prudence and good government left a rich treasury. He was said to have accumulated an army of 180,000 men and had 20,000 pieces of cannon and 3,600 elephants. Having these resources at his command, Daud determined to try his strength with the emperor. He began by attacking the imperial garrison and destroying the fort of Patna.

When this news reached Akbar, he sent a *firman* from Delhi to Khan Khanan (Commander-in-chief) Munim Khan, ordering him to punish Daud and to subdue Behar. Munim made peace with Daud's governor of Behar, which Akbar did not like. He therefore sent Raja Todar Mall Khetri to supersede Munim. Meanwhile Daud had taken refuge in the fort of Hajipur to which the imperial forces laid siege. Akbar on hearing this embarked and sailed for Patna; but on his arrival, determined first to reduce Hajipur. A force of 3,000 men were sent over and Raja Gajpati, *Zemindar* of Hajipur, was ordered to support the troops. The rebels were defeated; Fathe Khan Barha, Commander of the fort, was slain with many of his soldiers and their heads were sent to Daud, in order that he might reflect on his position. The latter indeed did take fright and fled to Bengal. On his way to Tandah, Daud left orders that the strong fort at Rajmahal with the pass of Teliagarhi should be strongly garrisoned and defended to the last extremity.

But seeing that the king himself had fled to Tandah, and taking fright at the fate of the garrison of Hajipur, the garrison of Rajmahal quietly submitted to Munim Khan. Daud on hearing this fled to Orissa. Raja Todar Mall was sent after Daud into Orissa, and was soon after joined by Munim Khan. Early in 1574, a great battle took place near Takaroi or Mughalmari north of Jaleswar in Balasor, in which Daud was completely defeated. After the battle, Munim advanced upon Cuttack in pursuit of Daud, where a peace was concluded. Daud renounced all claims to Bengal and Behar, in return for which he received the Province of Orissa, as a fief from the Mughal Emperor. Upon the death of Munim Khan, however, in the following year, Daud revolted and overran Bengal with his troops. The emperor appointed Husain Kuli Khan as Munim's successor, and Raja Todar Mall as next in command. They carried their army against Daud and commenced the siege of his entrenchments at Agmahal. The Afghans were again defeated in 1576, in the great battle of Agmahal (Rajmahal). Daud Khan was slain, and two years later, Orissa became a Province of Akbar's empire. With Daud the power of the Afghans ended.

Depopulation of Gaur.—Munim Khan after his return from Orissa, occupied the already decaying city of Gaur. He resolved to maintain Gaur as the seat of government and to restore its former magnificence. But very soon a mysterious pestilence broke out amongst the troops and the inhabitants. Thousands died every day and the living tired of burying the dead, threw them into the river without distinction of Hindu and Muhammadan. Munim himself fell a victim to the contagion. Henceforth the name of Gaur is scarcely to be found in the Muhammadan annals, and it is supposed that the city was never re-occupied after this depopulation. The city is now in ruins and filled with impenetrable jungles. It is now the abode of tigers and wild beasts. The date of the catastrophe, to which it would be hard to find a parallel in the history of civilization, was 1575 A. D.

General Remarks on the Afghan Rule.—The Afghan rule in Bengal extended for more than three hundred and fifty years, from the year in which Baktiar Khiliji first conquered it till the year in which it passed into the hands of the Mughals. During these four centuries, though for only forty years the Hindu king Ganes and his successors, and for seven years the Abyssinians ruled the province, the other kings were all Afghans. They gradually extended their dominions over the whole of Bengal and Behar with the exception of Bishnupur and Panchakot on the west, the kingdoms lying on the borders of Sunderbans on the south, Chattagram (Chittagong), Noakhali and Tripura on the east, and Kuch Behar on the north. Though they made repeated attempts to conquer Orissa, the excellent feudal organization of the Province, turned back the tide of their invasion and drove them into the heart of Bengal.

Their government was conducted in the following way. The ruler selected certain portion of the kingdom for his own domain, the rest was divided among his chiefs, who divided the lands among their dependents. They were allowed a portion of the rent to keep up a certain number of troops and support themselves, and the rest they remitted to the royal treasury. The majority of the Hindu landholders were deprived of their lands and reduced to much poverty. These chiefs and landholders were required to keep order in their respective lands and to maintain the police. They had the powers for the apprehension of offenders and the settlement of the village lands. All questions of the village communities were settled by them. The mass of the general people were at the mercy of these chiefs and landholders, and consequently it cannot be considered they were prosperous and in peace. They were always oppressed for money, and the frequent wars that occurred added to their misery. The king and his courtiers however lived in a state of comfort and luxury. Gaur, Panduah and Tandan or Tangra were made capital cities or the seats of government by different kings and each was adorned with splendid buildings. These magnificent edifices prove that the art of buildings rose to its highest perfection at the time. Many fine tanks were dug and *sarais* and splendid roads were constructed for the convenience of travellers.

The religion of the Hindus suffered much in the hands of the Afghans. Their temples were destroyed and idols demolished and mosques raised on their sites. Many of the Hindus were by force converted to Muhammadanism.

During the Afghan rule Brahmanism made a conquest over Buddhism. The great Vishnuvite reformation took place at this time. The sect was founded by Chaitanya, who was born at Nadiya in 1485 A. D. of Brahman parents. His father's name was Jagannath Misra and that of his mother Sachi Devi. He lost his father when a child and continued to live at home till he attained the age of twenty-four. He then went on a pilgrimage to Mathura and Jagannath and became a worshipper of Krishna. 'He then promulgated his doctrines, denouncing the caste system, and asserting that religion consisted not in worshipping the Diety according to special ritual, but in loving God—the Diety to be meditated on by the inward soul.' For simplicity and purity of character, he was probably unrivalled among the Hindu religious reformers. Chaitanya, after a life of forty-eight years, disappeared from the world in 1533 A. D.

Smarta Bhattacharjya Siromani was a contemporary of Chaitanya. They were both pupils of Basudev Sarbabhauma. Smarta Bhattacharjya is the author of *Astabinshati Tattwa*, which prescribes the rules still observed in the Durga Pujah, marriage, *sradha*, investiture of the holy thread and other ceremonies. The renowned doctor of Logic, Raghu Siramani flourished at this time. He is the author of the celebrated work on Logic the *Chintamani Didhiti*. Rup and Sanatan the principal disciples of Chaitanya wrote many Sanskrit works. The early Bengali poets Chandidas and Bidyapati flourished in this period. Chandidas was born at a village named Nannur in Birbhum, and Bidyapati in Mithila. Many social reforms took place among the Hindus during the Afghan rule. Udayana Acharjya Bhaduri divided the Barendras into eight septs or *patis*. Devibar Ghattak subdivided the Rarhi Brahmans into families or *mels*. Purandar Basu made rules of marriage among the Rarhi Kayasthas and Raja Paramananda Rai of Chandradip similarly made rules regarding Bangaja Kayasthas.

CHAPTER VIII.

THE MUGHAL SUBADARS OF BENGAL.

Husain Kuli Khan (1576—1578.)—After the battle of Agmahal, Husain Kuli Khan who got the title of Khan Jahan from the emperor again defeated the Pathans. He subdued Behar and occupied the strong fort of Rhotasghar. A force was sent to Orissa to seize the property of the late Raja, and Kuch Behar was compelled to pay tribute. Thus before his death in 1578 A. D. the whole of Bengal, Behar and Orissa became a Mughal Province.

Muzaffar Khan (1578—1580.)—The emperor Akbar appointed Muzaffar Khan to succeed Khan Jahan.

Rebellion of the Jaigirdars.—At this time occurred the rebellion of the Mughal *Jaigirdars*, which grew so furious that the throne of Akbar began to tremble. After the

Afghans were driven out, many of the Mughal officers took possession of their estates, which they occupied as *Jaigirdars*. These *Jaigirdars* were required to keep a certain number of troops to defend the king in time of need, and to make over the surplus revenues of their estates to the imperial treasury, after defraying the expenses for the maintenance of themselves and of their troops. When the Mughal *Jaigirdars* were called on to pay the balances of their estates, they rose in open rebellion and at once seized the capital of Bengal. The Mughal *Jaigirdars* of Behar also rose in rebellion for the same reason and took possession of the country. Muzaffar Khan, at this crisis, shut himself up in the fort of Tandah, but the rebels captured him and put him to death, and for a short period became masters of Bengal.

Raja Todar Mall (1580—1581.)—At this crisis the Emperor Akbar sent Raja Todar Mall as Subadar of Bengal and Behar, and he came down with a body of Rajput troops to crush the revolt. The Raja acted with great spirit and wisdom. He prevailed on all the Hindu Zemindars not to supply provisions to the rebels, who failing to cope with him, immediately abandoned the province. They took refuge in the frontier districts of Orissa and Dacca. At Dacca they established themselves and erected forts at Ganakpara and Guripara near Dhamrai. Todar Mall failed, however to work in harmony with the Mughal chiefs, who grew jealous of him. He represented his case to the Emperor, who recalled him and put Aziz Khan in his place as Subadar with the title of Khan Azam.

The Rent-roll of Todar Mall.—After his return from Behar, Todar Mall was appointed to the Finance Ministership of the empire, for which his name is so very famous. He prepared his rent-roll a copy of which is preserved in the *Ain-i-Akbari*. His rent-roll was completed about 1582 A. D. and it remained in force till 1658 A. D. In his rent-roll, which is called *Asl-i-Jama Tumar*, Bengal Proper is divided into 19 *sarkars* containing 689 *mahals*. The revenue from land, salt, fisheries, and port-dues amounted to 1,06,93,067 *Akhbarshahi* rupees, exclusive of the family subsistence or *nankar* of the collectors of revenue which amounted to Rs. 3,26,250. Behar was divided into 7 *sarkars* and 200 *mahals* and its revenue was fixed at Rs. 55,47,985. Orissa was divided into 5 *sarkars* and 99 *mahals* and its revenue amounted to Rs. 42,68,330.

Aziz Khan (1581—1589.)—The first endeavour of the new Subadar was to put down the rebels. He created dissensions among the chief of the Jaigirdars, by sowing seeds of jealousy and succeeded in subduing them. He took quiet possession of Tandah but he was soon required to go to Agra. Two Subadars were appointed to succeed him but they failed to crush the rebellion. One of them Shahbaz Khan, who was Subadar only for a few months, purchased peace by giving up the whole of Orissa to the Afghans on condition that they should not molest Bengal in future.

Raja Man Sing (1589—1605.)—The Afghans however did not long remain quiet, and in A. D. 1589 Akbar sent Raja Man Sing the celebrated Rajput as Subadar. In the beginning Man Sing was not successful, and his son Jagat Sing fell into the hands of the Afghans. But fortunately Kutlu Khan the chief of the rebels died. The Afghans sent back Jagat Sing and proposed for peace. A peace was concluded on condition that the Afghans should strike the coin in Emperor's name, and give up the temple of Jagannath at Puri to Man Sing. Two years afterwards the Afghan chiefs under Osman again rebelled, seized and plundered the temple of Jagannath. Man Sing without losing a moment's time marched into Orissa. He completely defeated the rebels in a great battle on the banks of the river Subarnarekha, captured all forts and strongholds, and finally re-included it in the rent-roll of the empire in 1592. From that year the imperial commissions (*Sanads*) appointing a Governor of the Lower Provinces, regularly include 'Bengal, Behar, and Orissa'.

Rajmahal made capital.—Returning from Orissa, Man Sing made Agmahal his capital and gave it the name of Rajmahal. He commenced to build not only a palace for himself but also a Hindu temple. Fateh-Jang Khan, the Musulman Governor of Behar, who had lived at Rajmahal before the Rajput General's arrival, wrote to the Emperor that Man Sing was building a temple for idolatrous worship and evidently meditated insurrection. Man Sing, hearing of this, changed the name of the town from Rajmahal to Akbarnagar and turned the temple into the *Juma Masjid*.

Kuch Behar made tributary.—In A. D. 1595 Man Sing married the sister of the Raja of Kuch Behar, who professed himself the vassal of the Emperor of Delhi. For this the relatives and courtiers of the Kuch Behar

Raja rose up against him. Man Sing sent an army and restored him to the Rajdom. This was the first time that the Mughals entered the kingdom of Kuch Behar and made it tributary.

Rebellion of the Afghans under Osman.—Man Sing was soon after obliged to leave Bengal to join the Mughal army which was engaged in the Dakshin. During his absence he left his son Jagat Sing as his deputy. Osman the chief of the Afghans in Orissa, no sooner heard of this than he revolted, defeated the imperial army and conquered the greater part of Bengal. Man Sing hastened back to Bengal, collected his troops in the strong fort at Rhotasghar and marched against the Afghans. He met the enemy at Sherpur a place between Bardwan and Murshidabad and totally routed them. Osman fled to Orissa.

Man Sing's power.—Man Sing now governed Bengal in peace for a space of fifteen years, and became very powerful. He had in his pay twenty thousand troops and was considered the head of the Hindus throughout the Empire.

Hearing that the Emperor Akbar was about to die, he resigned his governorship and returned to Agra. His object was to try if he could secure the imperial throne for his nephew Prince Khasru. Akbar's son Prince Salim married the sister of Man Sing and Prince Khasru was the offspring. Man Sing however could not accomplish his purpose, and Salim succeeded in 1605 under the title of Emperor Jahangir. Though Man Sing had opposed Jahangir, the latter was afraid of his power and in order to keep him away from the imperial court, again appointed him Governor of Bengal; but he was within eight months recalled to make room for Kutab-ud-din.

The Twelve Bhuians.—It is supposed that at this time, there were in East Bengal, twelve Zemindars who were very powerful. They were called twelve *Bhuians*. Protapaditya of Yasohara, Mukunda Rai of Bhusna, Kandarpya Narayan Rai of Chandradwip, Laksman Manik of Bhulua, Kedar Rai of Bikrampur, Fazal Gazi of Bhowal, Isa Khan of Khijirpur, Raja Ramkrishna of Satail, Chand Gazi of Chand Protap were nine of them. Some say that the Rajas of Putia, Tahirpur and Dinajpur completed the twelve.

Raja Protapaditya.—Of these Raja Protapaditya was the most powerful and he humbled the rest. He defied even the authority of the Emperor and refused tribute. He was an usurper, having banished the rightful Raja Kachu Rai. Kachu Rai proceeded to Delhi for the purpose of moving the Emperor to recognise his claim to the Yasohara Raj. The Emperor after being satisfied with his claim sent Man Sing to bring the rebel Raja to subjection. On the arrival of Man Sing at Chakdah, Majmuadar* Bhabanand the ancestor of the present Maharaja of Krishnagar supplied him with provisions and gave him assistance in every way, and even accompanied him to the capital of Protapaditya. Protapaditya defended himself boldly; but after showing a great deal of courage, was overcome. His fort was stormed and he was captured. He was shut up in an iron cage to be taken up to Delhi, but he died on the way at Benares. Man Sing presented the Majmuadar to the Emperor

* Corrupted in Bengali into *Majumdar*.

Jahangir, and brought to his Majesty's notice the services rendered by him in the expedition against Protapaditya. The Emperor restored him to his raj and conferred on him the title of Maharaja.

Kutab-ud-din Khan (1606—1607.)—The object of Emperor Jahangir to recall Man Sing was to serve his own motive. When a prince, Jahangir was smitten with the charms of a very beautiful girl named Meherunnesa and wished to marry her; but as she was betrothed to Sher Afghan, Akbar disapproved of the marriage.

Sher Khan.—She became the wife of Sher, who finding his life not safe at Delhi, went away with his wife to Bengal, having been appointed Chief of Bardwan. Jahangir, now Lord of India, still hoped to get the lady at all hazards. He knew that Man Sing, his brother-in-law, would not assist him to gain his ends and so sent Kutab-ud-din in 1606 as Governor of Bengal, with secret orders to bring Meherunnesa to the imperial harem. Kutab went to Bardwan and Sher came to receive him. On some pretence or other Kutab brought about a scuffle between himself and Sher. The latter understood that they wanted his life and so determined to die like a brave man, as indeed he was. He mortally wounded Kutab and killed five other nobles who advanced to attack him. At last the men arround him showered their arrows and bullets from a distance and he fell. The scene of the encounter is still pointed out at Sadhinpur, east of the Bardwan railway station. The widow of Sher Afghan was soon after sent to Delhi and she became the wife of Jahangir with the well known title of Nur Jahan.

Islam Khan (1607—1613.)—After Kutab-ud-din's

death Jahangir Kuli Khan was appointed Subadar of Bengal. In 1607, he defeated and slew the famous Raja Sankar Ram of Gorakpur. Nothing more is known of him than the cruel rigour with which he collected his revenues. He was succeeded by Islam Khan.

Revolt of the Afghans again.—At this time the Afghans again revolted. Osman Khan, their chief collected an army of 20,000 men and was proclaimed king. He overran the lower part of Bengal and maintained his position till 1612. Islam Khan sent against him his brave and experienced general Shujat Khan and in a battle in Eastern Bengal, Osman was defeated and slain by the Mughals.

Dacca made capital.—After this victory Islam Khan removed the seat of government from Rajmahal to Dacca. Prior to that time, the eastern capital of the Mughal Provincial administration was Sonargaon. The cause of the transfer is mentioned to have been the descent of the Maghs and the distress caused by the Portuguese pirates on the coasts of Bengal. Islam Khan erected there a fort, increased the strength of the fleet and artillery and changed the name of the town to Jahangirnagar or Jahangirabad.

The Portuguese in Bengal.—The Portuguese made their first appearance in Bengal about the end of the sixteenth century. They were then in the employ of the Raja of Arakan, holding high commands and possessing extensive grants of land. In 1607 they offended the Raja of Arakan and many were put to death. A number of them escaped in nine or ten small vessels and betook themselves to piracy at the mouths of the Megna. The

Mughal Governor of Sandwip, Fathe Khan sent an expedition of forty vessels and six hundred soldiers against the pirates. His fleet found the Portuguese anchored off the island of Daksin Shahbazpur and proceeded to attack them; but the superior skill of the Portuguese in the management of their ships and in the use of their cannon gave them the victory, the engagement ending in Fathe Khan and the greater part of his troops being killed, and all his ships captured. Gonzales, the Portuguese leader became master of the island. He had under his command 1000 Portuguese, 2000 Indian soldiers, 200 cavalry and 80 vessels well armed with cannon, with which he seized Daksin Shahbazpur and Patelbanga. In 1610 an alliance was formed by the Raja of Arakan and the Portuguese to invade Bengal, the former by land and the latter by sea under the command of Gonzales. At first they met with little opposition and both Lakshimpur and Bhulua in the District of Noakhali fell into their hands. But they were afterwards defeated by the Mughal troops and pursued nearly as far as Chittagong.

Kasim Khan (1613—1618.)—Islam Khan was succeeded in the Viceroyalty by his brother Kasim Khan in 1613. From this period to the accession of Sultan Muhammad Shuja to the viceroyalty of the Subah, in 1639, the country appears to have been desolated by continual internal wars and foreign incursions by the Assamese in the north and the Maghs and the Portuguese in the south. Subsequently a quarrel arose between the Raja of Arakan and Gonzales; and in a severe fight the commander of the Portuguese was slain, and the Raja of

Arakan in the following year took possession of the island of Sandwip. For failing to bring order into the country, the Emperor Jahangir deposed Kasim Khan and appointed Ibrahim Khan, the brother of Nur Jahan to the Subadari of Bengal and Orissa in the year 1618.

Ibrahim Khan (1618—1624.)—During the first five year's of Ibrahim's rule, Bengal enjoyed peace and prosperity. Manufacture and trade were encouraged. The delicate muslins of Dacca and the silks of Maldah were brought to perfection. The internal administration was also ably conducted. The Assamese had been repelled; the Arakanese were driven off; and the Afghans in Orissa were completely subdued.

Rebellion of Shah Jahan.—Unfortunately at this time Prince Shah Jahan revolted against his father, the Emperor Jahangir; and the event filled the country with bloodshed and misery. In the battle which ensued between the father and the son, Shah Jahan was defeated and obliged to fly to the Daksin. His elder brother pursued him but he suddenly turned off and entered Bardwan. He asked aid from the Portuguese Governor but was refused. Shah Jahan overran Bengal and proceeded to Rajmahal. Ibrahim Khan advanced to meet him. A severe battle ensued, in which Ibrahim was defeated and slain. Shah Jahan then proceeded to Dacca and collected from the treasury forty *laks* of Rupees. He remained two years in possession of the country and after regulating its affairs marched towards Delhi. He successively took Monghyr, Patna and Rhotas, in which latter place he kept his family for security. The imperial army approached and a bloody battle was fought on the banks of the Tons. Shah Jahan was completely defeated and pursued from place to place. He at last threw himself upon the mercy of his father, who forgave him.

The reigns of next three Governors.—The short reigns of the next three Governors Khanezad Khan, Makram Khan, Fidai Khan, extending from 1624 to 1628 were uneventful.

Kasim Khan Juwaini (1628—1632.)—When after the death of Jahangir, Shah Jahan became Emperor, he sent in 1628 Kasim Khan Juwaini as his Viceroy to Bengal.

Massacre of the Portuguese.—From a very early period the Portuguese had established themselves at Satgaon and built fort and churches and largely extended their power. Kasim reported to the Emperor that the Portuguese had grown very insolent, that they levied tolls on boats which passed by their factory, that they committed piracies at the mouths of rivers, and that they were in the habit of converting natives to their religion by force. The Emperor ordered the Subadar to expel the Portuguese from his dominions. In 1632 the Mughal army laid siege to Hugli, which lasted for three months. The Portuguese for several months defended themselves boldly and also offered to pay a tribute of a *lak* of Rupees but it was rejected. The Mughals at last dug a mine under the place and blew it up. They then butchered the Portuguese without mercy and destroyed the place entirely. One thousand Portuguese fell in the seige and four thousand and four hundred men, women and children became captives. The most beautiful women were sent to the seraglio of Shah Jahan. Satgaon was hence reduced to an obscure village.

Hugli made a royal port.—Hugli was made a royal port and a *fousdar* or military commander was appointed for the place. Kasim Khan died in 1632.

Islam Khan Mushaddi (1637—1639.)—Kasim Khan was succeeded by Azim Khan who was found quite unequal to defend the Province from the invasions of the Maghs and Assamese. He was consequently superseded by Islam Khan Mushaddi.

Raja of Arakan became vassal of the Delhi Emperor.—In 1638 A. D. Matak Rai one of the Magh chiefs, who held Chittagong on the part of the Raja of Arakan, having incurred the displeasure of his prince and being apprehensive of punishment, sought the protection of the Mughals and acknowledged himself a vassal of the Delhi Emperor. Islam Khan accepted the offer, and changed the name of the town to Islamabad. But it was not till 1666 or nearly thirty years later, that Chittagong could be incorporated into the Mughal Empire.

Assam captured and plundered.—During the same year, the Raja of Assam came down with a large number of men and boats, plundering the villages and towns that fell in his way and had nearly reached Dacca, when the Subadar went out and met him with boats armed with cannon. The Raja of Assam was completely defeated and Islam Khan pursued him into his own country and captured fifteen forts and much spoil. It was during his reign which extended for the space of a year that Kuch Behar was invaded by the Muhammadans.

Sultan Shuja (1639—1660.)—In 1639 A. D. Islam

Khan was recalled to Agra to take the post of Vazir of the Mughal Empire; and Sultan Shuja, the second son of the Emperor Shah Jahan was appointed Subadar of Bengal. Behar was made a separate government. His first act was to transfer the capital of Bengal from Dacca to Rajmahal, which he fortified and adorned with splendid buildings. After having governed Bengal with credit for eight years, he was recalled through the jealousy and fears of his father and made governor of Cabul, but within two years he was restored to the Subadarship of Bengal. During his reign the English obtained a firm footing as traders in Bengal.

The East India Company (1600—1642.)—In the year 1600 in the reign of Queen Elizabeth, a company of merchants was formed in England to trade in the East. This company was the East India Company. They paid a tax to the Queen and Parliament, and the Queen promised to protect them, and not allow any nation with which England was at war to hurt or destroy their towns where they had their trade, or their ships when they were carrying goods from place to place. They traded at first in the west coast of India and the Eastern Archipelago. The earliest settlement in Eastern India was at Pipli, on the Subarnarekha, established in 1634. The permission of establishing a factory at Balasor was acquired for the East India Company by a Mr. Gabriel Broughton. This gentleman in 1636 had the good fortune to cure a daughter of the Emperor, whose clothes had caught fire; and in 1640 he successfully treated one of the ladies of the Bengal Viceroy's Zenana. When asked to name his own reward, he begged that his countrymen might be allowed a maritime settlement in Bengal. Accordingly the imperial commission was issued, granting the English a land factory at Hugli and a maritime settlement at Balasor with power to export and import goods free of duty. This was in 1642.

Rent-roll of Shuja.—The rent-roll of Todar Mall was revised during the regency of Sultan Shuja. A short time before 1658 he fixed the revenue at Rs. 1,31,15,907 being an increase of 24 *laks* on the *Asl Jama* of Todar Mall. Shuja's rent-roll gave Bengal wider limits. Hijili, Midnapur, Jaleswar, portions of Kuch Behar, Western Assam and Tipperah were added to Bengal partly as newly conquered territory. Several Chiefs of Chutia Nagpur also paid tribute, and portions of the Sundarbans, if not actually reclaimed, were for the first time assessed. Altogether his roll showed 34 *sarkars*, consisting of 1350 *mahals* or *parganas*.

Shuja's aspiration to the Delhi Throne and his end.—The prosperous reign of Sultan Shuja was soon after changed into one of war and misery. In 1657 the Emperor Shah Jahan fell dangerously ill, and his four sons Dara, Shuja, Aurangzeb and Murad began to aspire to the throne. Shuja as Subadar of Bengal, having large resources at his command, immediately prepared to secure the throne for himself. He marched with his army to Benares and was met by the son of Dara, Prince Saliman and general Jai Sing and while negotiations for a treaty were going on, the prince took him by surprise and Shuja was obliged to fly, first to Patna and then to Monghyr. Saliman hastened to besiege the place but was recalled by his father to fight his two uncles Murad and Aurangzeb. Dara was defeated, the old Emperor Shah Jahan was thrown into prison and Aurangzeb ascended the throne of Delhi. When events thus transpired, Shuja offered congratulations to his brother and asked to be confirmed in the governorship of Bengal. The brother replied that as he had been the regent of his father, no new confirmation was necessary. In the meantime Shuja collected an army and made another attempt for the throne. Near Allahabad another battle was fought with the imperial forces under Aurangzeb and his General Mir Jumla. Shuja was again defeated and fled first to Patna and then to Monghyr. Aurangzeb sent his son Prince Muhammad with Mir Jumla in pursuit of him. Shuja fled to Rajmahal where he defended himself for six days, and thence fled to Tandah. Here Prince Muhammad who was smitten with the charms of Shuja's daughter, suddenly left his own army and joined Shuja. Mir Jumla however, fought a decisive battle, outside the walls of Tandah. Shuja and Muhammad, utterly routed, fled to Dacca. Shuja was ultimately driven from Bengal and he took refuge in Arakan. There at last he was shamefully treated by the Arakan Raja. He was taken prisoner and drowned 1651 A. D. His wife and two daughters committed suicide and another daughter was forcibly married to the Arakan Raja. Thus ended Shuja the most beloved Subadar of Bengal.

Mir Jumla (1660—1664.)—At his accession in 1660 Mir Jumla, once more made Dacca the seat of his government. To guard against the incursions of the *Maghs* and other frontier tribes from Arakan, Mir Jumla built several forts at the confluence of Lahkmia and Dhalesvari the ruins of which still remain. The principal of these are the forts of Hajiganj and Idrakpur, the latter of which has now been converted into a residence for the Deputy Magistrate of Munshiganj. He also constructed several good military roads and bridges in the vicinity of the city of Dacca, and the bridges at Pagla and Tungi are attributed to him. The former of these is now in ruins, the latter was blown up during mutiny by Mr. Carnac, the Magistrate. Mir Jumla undertook an expedition into Assam, having first overrun Kuch Behar and seized its capital which he named Alamgirnagar in honor of his master Aurangzeb whose another name was Alamgir. He obtained a series of successes in Assam but was ultimately obliged to retreat on account of disease among his troops. He himself fell sick and died near Dacca.

Shaistah Khan (1664—1689.)—Mir Jumla was succeeded by Shaista Khan Amir ul Omra, nephew of the Empress Nur Jahan. One of the first measures undertaken by him was an expedition against Chittagong, which was captured and whose name was changed to Islamabad—the Residence of the Faithful—and annexed to the Province of Bengal. Shaista Khan ruled fifteen years, with a break of two years, during which Fidai Khan, Azim Khan and Sultan Muhammad Azam, third son of Aurangzeb, acted as viceroys. The period of his government was noted as one of general tranquility and prosperity. It is said that rice sold at this time at eight *mans* for the rupee. The English settled in Dacca about 1660, and about 1666 the Dacca muslins were first introduced into England.

The East India Company (1642—1696.)—Up to the reign of Shaista Khan the trade of the East India Company flourished in Bengal. The French, the Dutch and the Danes with a view to participate in Bengal-trade made settlements at Chandarnagar, Chinsura and Serampore respectively. In 1677 the English merchants through the influence of Shaista Khan obtained a perpetual *firman* from the Emperor Aurangzeb to trade in Bengal by an annual payment of 3,000 rupees. They then possessed extensive factories at Hugli, Patna, Dacca, Balasor, Maldah and Kasimbazar. The Court of Directors then made the factories of Bengal independent of Madras and Mr. Hodges was appointed its first chief. He was allowed a guard of a corporal and twenty European soldiers. In order to prevent the intrusion of private merchants, the chief asked permission to erect a fort at the mouth of the Hugli river but Shaista Khan refused. There were also at this time several disturbances in Behar, during which the English factory at Patna remained uninjured; and therefore the Subadar suspected that the English were implicated in the rebellion. The Subadar, then contrary to the stipulations of the *firman*, imposed a duty of 3½ per cent. on their goods.

In 1685 the oppressions and exactions of the Mughal Subadar drove the English into open hostilities, and from then till 1688 the English waged rather an unsuccessful war against the Mughals. In 1686 Shaista Khan issued orders confiscating all the English factories in Bengal. The merchants at Hugli, under their president Job Charnock retreated to a place 26 miles down Sutanuti, now the northern quarter of the town of Calcutta. Early in February 1687, a large army came to Hugli to expel the English. In 1688, Captain Heath who commanded the Company's forces determined to quit Bengal altogether. He accordingly embarked with all the Company's servants and goods from their fenceless factories, sailed down the Hugli and anchored at Balasor. When attacked by the Musalman governor, he burned the town. He also made an unsuccessful attempt on Chittagong and then without waiting for a treaty with the Subadar, sailed away to Madras. It was about this time that Shaista Khan also resigned the government of Bengal.

Ibrahim Khan (1689—1697.)—Shaista Khan was succeeded in the government of Bengal by Ibrahim Khan, in 1689.

Revival of the Company's trade in Bengal.— In the following year he was directed by the Emperor to invite the English back to Bengal. The reason was that the English captured every vessel, which left the shores of India and so the voyage of pilgrims to Mecca was interrupted. Mr. Charnock returned to Sutanuti with all English merchants and officers. In the next year he received the imperial order to carry on trade free of all duties, except the annual payment of a *pesh kash* of Rupees 3,000. Twice during the next four years the trade of the English in Bengal was ordered by the Emperor to be stopped but the favour of Ibrahim Khan enabled them to carry it on. Once in 1692 it was stopped at the request of the Sultan of Turkey, who asked the Emperor to prevent the Europeans to trade in saltpetre; for with it they made gunpowder to fight against his

Muhammadan subjects. For the second time again in 1695 when Captain Kyd, an English pirate captured a number of Mughal ships, containing pilgrims bound for Mecca, the Emperor avenged himself by retarding English trade to a large extent.

Rebellion of Subha Sing.—The English merchants in Bengal were always anxious to build a fortress for their security, but the Mughal government would not permit them. At length in 1696 an event occurred which enabled them to fortify their factories. Subha Sing, *talukdar* of Chitwa and Barda, then a part of Burdwan, raised the standard of rebellion against the empire. Rahim Khan, an Afghan chief co-operated with him in the insurrection. In a stand-up fight they slew the Maharaja of Bardwan, Kishna Ram Rai, and captured all the members of his family except his son Jagat Rai, who went to Dacca to seek assistance from the Governor. Subha Sing was stabbed and slain by a daughter of the Maharaja, when he attempted to outrage her person. The insurgents continued the revolt, captured Hugli but was forced to retire by the Governor of Chinsurah.

Fort William erected.—The English at Sutanuti, the French at Chandarnagar, and the Dutch at Chinsurah applied to the Subadar to be allowed to put their factories in a state of defence, against the attack of the rebels. Their application was granted. With great pleasure the English commenced to build their fort, which they named Fort William after the name of William the Third, the then reigning king of England.

The rebellion checked.—The insurgents plundered Nadiya and Murshidabad under Rahim Khan, whom they elected as their chief, after the death of Subha Singh. Owing to the extreme apathy of Ibrahim, Rahim became master of all Western Bengal from Rajmahal to Midnapur. At length the emperor superseded him and appointed his grandson Prince Azim-u-shan Governor of Bengal. But before the arrival of the Prince, a brave son of Ibrahim named Zabardast Khan defeated the rebels in a battle near Rajmahal A.D. 1697. But the insurrection was not totally suppressed till 1698, when Rahim Khan was defeated and slain in a battle near Bardwan. Of his followers some were slain and some entered the service of the Prince.

Sultan Azim-u-shan (1697—1706).—During the reign of this Subadar, in A. D. 1698 the Company got permission to purchase the *talukdari* right to the villages of Sutanuti, Gobindapur, and Calcutta, corresponding to the existing site of the city of palaces, subject to an annual revenue of Rs. 495.

United East India Company.—About the same year a new English Company started to trade in the East. The rivalry of the two companies was injurious to both and so the two companies were united under the name of 'United East India Company.' The garrison of Fort William was then increased by 130 European soldiers.

Murshid Kuli Khan.—The name of Murshid Kuli Khan has a close connection with the reign of this Subadar. He was the son of a poor Brahman, and when young was taken as a slave to Persia and there brought up in the Muhammadan faith. At different times of his life he passed by different names. The name he received from his master was Muhammad Hadi. In English books he is called Jaffier Khan. After the foundation of Murshidabad, he obtained from the Emperor Aurangzeb, the lofty title of Nawab Murshid Kuli, Mutamin-ul-Mulk, Ala-ud-Daula, Jafar Khan Nasiri, Nasir Jang—meaning the viceroy, the priest-slave, the administrator of the country, the lofty one of the empire, Lord Jafar Nasari, the victorious in war.

Murshid Kuli Khan at first entered an insignificant service, but by his talent and energy became Dewan of Haidrabad. When Azim-u-Shan was appointed, the office of *Nizam* was given to him and Murshid was appointed *Dewan*. The duty of *Nizam* was to defend and govern the Province and to enforce laws; the *Dewan* was to collect and disburse revenues. Murshid Kuli Khan went to Dacca and in various ways increased the revenue of the Province so much that he rose high in the estimation of the Emperor, but fell in the bad graces of the Nizam who conspired to take his life. They openly quarrelled with each other, but the Emperor took the side of Murshid Kuli Khan, and severely reprimanded his grandson. He directed him to leave Bengal and go to Behar. Murshid Kuli Khan also resolved not to live at Dacca and took up his abode at Muksudabad where he removed the seat of government. In the second year of his appointment A.D. 1703, Murshid Kuli Khan prepared the accounts of revenues and presented them to the Emperor in the Daksin. He was so much delighted that he made him Deputy Nazim for Bengal and Orissa.

Prince Azim-u-shan left Bengal in 1706 and since then

he was mostly occupied in securing the Imperial throne for his father Bahadur Shah. Murshid Kuli Khan was the real Governor of Bengal. The Prince left his son Farrukh Siyyar as his deputy at Murshidabad but he did not in any way interfere with state affairs. When Farrukh Siyyar became Emperor of Delhi, Murshid Kuli Khan gained absolute power in Bengal. Dacca ceased to be the seat of the viceregal government, and the eastern Districts were made over to a Naib or Deputy of the Nazim. The *naibat* extended from the Garo hills on the north to the Sunderbans on the south, and from the Tipperah hills on the east to Jessore on the west. It was considered the highest and most lucrative appointment under the Nizamat.

Calcutta declared a Presidency.—In 1707, Calcutta was declared a Presidency by the United Company. But it was dependent upon Madras, where there was a fort and garrison which the Company had not been allowed to maintain in Bengal.

CHAPTER IX.

THE NAWABS NAZIM OF BENGAL.

Murshid Kuli Khan (1712—1725).—After removing the seat of government to Muksudabad, Murshid Kuli Khan forthwith erected there a palace and several other offices of government. He also established an imperial mint from which came out most of the Shah Alam gold *mohurs* now to be found in the *basars*.

His Rule.—Murshid Kuli Khan ruled at Murshidabad in almost undisturbed quiet, virtually from 1704 till his death in 1725. This period falls within the reigns of three emperors each of whom confirmed him in his rank and power. In 1713 he received from Prince Farrukh Siyyar the united offices of *Nazim* and *Dewan*. In 1718 he obtained from the same emperor the patent, conferring upon him the government of Behar in addition.

He ruled the Province with efficiency. He provided against famine, by prohibiting the monopoly and exportation of grain. Rice commonly sold at Murshidabad at 4 *mans* for a rupee. He was indefatigable in the extirpation of robbers. Travellers were protected in the roads and every man slept securely in his house. He was impartial in his decisions and rigid in the execution of the sentence of law. He put his own son to death for an infraction of a certain law of the country. He devoted two days in the week to the administration of justice. In the collection of revenues his severity was dreaded. He always treated the Hindus with bigoted cruelty. To raise his own tomb, he pulled down all the Hindu temples in the neighbourhood and used their materials for its construction.

His Financial Reforms.—Murshid Kuli Khan made financial reforms which consisted in the abolition of the Bengal contingent of household troops (3000 horse). He set on foot throughout the interior districts a *hastabud* investigation for the purpose of making a revised assessment. These reforms are embodied in the *Jama-Kamil Tumar*, or perfect rent-roll. According to it, Bengal was from 1722 newly arranged into 13 *chaklas*, subdivided into 1660 *parganas*, and was assessed of an annual revenue of Rs. 1,42,88,186. Two of the *chaklas* were annexations from Orissa, *viz.* Bandar Balasor and Hijli; five lay west of the Ganges, *viz.* Satgaon, Bardwan, Murshidabad, Jessore and Bhusna; and six lay north and east of the Ganges, *viz.* Akbarnagar, Goraghat, Karaibari, Jahangirnagar, Sylhet, and Islamabad. The *faujdaris* or magisterial jurisdictions coincided in area with the revenue *chaklas*. His other income from taxes called *abwab* amounted to more than a ½ laks.

Creation of Zemindars.—After the completion of his rent-roll, Murshid Kuli Khan removed the greater number of the old *Jaigirdars*, who were in his time simply the collectors of the dues of the state in the different *chaklas*. The Hindu Rajas of Dinajpur, Nadiya, Rajshahi and of other places were created by him. They gradually became rich and powerful, and their offices eventually became hereditary. Thus in 1725, Rajshahi, the most unweildy and extensive *Zemindari* in Bengal or perhaps in India, enclosing in its circuit the principal factories of Kasimbazar, Beauleah, Kumar Khali (Comer Colly) &c., was conferred on Ramjan, a Brahman, the first of the present family of Nattor. Dinajpur was, at the same time, placed in charge of Ramnath, an able landholder. Nadiya was entrusted to Ramjiban or more properly to his distinguished son Raghu Ram. But some difference was made in the case of the Birbhum and Bishnupur Rajas. Each of them was treated as an ally of the Nawab, with whom new arrangements were made for the payment of tribute.

His able Government.—Murshid Kuli Khan remitted every year to Delhi imperial revenue to the amount of one *kror* and fifty *laks* of rupees. Besides, he retained enormous sums for his own private use in the coffers of Jagat Seth at Murshidabad. During his time the Rajas of Tipperah, Kuch Behar, and Assam, whose countries had been overrun but never subdued by the Muhammadans, sent presents of submission to Murshidabad and acknowledged the nominal superiority of the Nawab. The only persons exempted from the payment of tribute were the *zemindars* of Birbhum and Bishnupur who retained their old character of feudatory chiefs.

New privileges conferred on the Company.—When Murshid Kuli became both *Nazim* and *Dewan*, he ordered the English merchants to pay the usual duties on their merchandise. So the East India Company sent an embassy to the Emperor Farrukh-Siyyar. Through the services of Surgeon Hamilton, who cured the Emperor of his sickness, the Company secured a *firman* by which they were allowed (1) to trade free of duty in Bengal; (2) to purchase the *talukdari* of 38 villages in the neighbourhood of Calcutta, subject to an annual revenue of Rs. 8,121; (3) to use the mint at Murshidabad three days in the week for the coinage of the English Company's money; (4) to have all persons indebted to the Company, delivered up by the Nawab's government. No other independent authority was conferred upon the Company, nor does any appear to have been claimed.

Murshid Kuli Khan's domestic affairs.—Murshid Kuli Khan endeavoured in every way to establish his own family in Bengal. His son-in-law Shuja-ud-daula was appointed Deputy Nazim of Orissa, and the husband of his grand-daughter was given the same office at Dacca. He nominated the son of Shuja-ud-daula to succeed him in the throne of Bengal and procured for him the title of Sarfaraz Khan. He purchased the *Zemindari* of the city of Murshidabad from the *talukdar* of Chunakhali and had the transfer registered in the books. He died in 1725 but the succession did not follow his last will.

Jagat Seth.—A short explanation of the term *Jagat Seth* will not be uninteresting. Manik Chand is regarded as the founder of the Seth family. When Murshid Kuli Khan, in 1704, transferred the capital to Murshidabad the banker followed him there and became the most influential personage in the new court. Manikchand was the right hand of the Nawab in all his financial reforms and also in his private affairs. The coffers of Manik Chand were the depository of the private hoards of the Nawab. In 1715 the Nawab secured for Manik Chand the title of *Seth* or banker. Manik Chand had no children and adopted his nephew Fathi Chand who received the title of *Seth*. When Fathi Chand first visited Delhi, the Emperor Muhammad Shah in 1724 conferred on him the title of *Jagat Seth* or the banker of the world. He was therefore the first of the family to bear the title of Jagat Seth which has become so well known in history.

Shuja-ud-Daula (1725-1739).—After the death of Murshid Kuli Khan, Shuja-ud-Daula or Shuja-ud-din, as he was sometimes called, managed to secure the vacant office for himself, through intrigues in the Delhi Court. His ancestors were originally Turkomans. He was himself born in the Daksin, where he early contracted an intimacy with Murshid Kuli Khan. He married the only daughter of the late Nawab and was the father of Sarfaraz Khan.

His Rule.—During his rule, the province of Tipperah, which had from time immemorial been an independent kingdom, was annexed to the Mughal Empire. Dinajpur and Kuch Behar were also invaded and the Rajas of those countries were plundered of their ancient treasures.

He appointed a Hindu named Rai Alam Chand to be an assistant to his son Sarfaraz Khan in the Dewanship of Bengal and procured for him the title of *Rai-Raian*. His most trusted advisers were the two brothers Haji Ahmad and Ali Vardi Khan, Alam Chand and Fathi Chand Jagat Seth.

Shuja-ud-Daula was liberal to his servants, and paid great attention to men of learning and piety; he was also very charitable. He was impartial in the administration of justice. He condemned to death the persons who were instruments of extortion during his predecessor's time. His collection of the revenues was as exact as that of his predecessor, but he was free from the reproach of cruelty and religious bigotry. He commenced his rule by releasing the unhappy *Zemindars*, imprisoned by his predecessor and permitting them to resume management of their estates, upon giving security for good conduct.

In the year 1728 he remitted to Delhi one *kror* and forty-eight *laks* of rupees. It is said that Suja-ud-Daula raised the taxes levied under the name of *abwab* to more than twenty laks of rupees or more than one-fifth of the original revenue. He raised the military establishment by an army of 25,000 men, half of whom were cavalry and half infantry. He embellished the city of Murshidabad; pulled down the palace of Murshid Kuli Khan and erected one more grand. His favorite residence was at Dehpara on the right bank of the Bhagirathi just opposite to Murshidabad. He completed a superb mosque in the midst of a beautiful garden to which he gave the name of Farah Bagh or the Garden of Beauty. He was buried there within a mausoleum erected by himself. After a peaceful rule of fourteen years he died in 1739.

Sarfaraz Khan (1739-1740).—During the first few years of his father's life, Sarfaraz Khan conducted the management of the state and succeeded to the Subah of Bengal without any disturbance. He does not appear to have ever received confirmation in the office from the Mughal Emperor, for at this time there were commotions and rebellions at Delhi. His father in his death-bed bound him to follow the instructions of his four councillors.

His weak character.,—The weakness of his character, however caused these powerful personages to turn into his enemies. He grossly insulted Fathi Chand Jagat Seth. His eldest son was married to a woman of exiquisite beauty, the report of which excited the curiosity of the Nawab to see her. No remonstrances succeeded to divert the will of the Nawab. The young woman was sent to the palace in the evening. She returned after a short stay in the palace, unviolated, but dishonored. The Jagat Seth then fell away from the Nawab and joined the adventurer Ali Verdi Khan. Ali Verdi Khan was at this time residing at Patna as Deputy-Governor of Behar. He took the lead in the conspiracy against the Nawab and gradually gathered a large number of troops. The ministers of the Emperor at Delhi were bribed to support the conspirators. In the year 1740, Ali Verdi Khan found himsef strong enough to revolt openly and to march into Bengal.

Battle of Gheria—After some treacherous negotiations, a battle was fought at Gheria on the Ganges about 22 miles from Murshidabad. Sarfaraz Khan was killed by a musket ball while fighting bravely from an elephant. This decided the event of the battle and Ali Verdi whose full name was Hassain-ul-Daula Ali Verdi Khan Mahabat Jang, took possession of the *masnad*.

Ali Verdi Khan (1740-1756).—After his accession to the throne of Bengal, Ali Verdi Khan found large accummulations in the treasury. He sent munificent presents to the Emperor and his courtiers and he was forthwith confirmed in the government of Bengal, Behar and Orissa. At this time the Mughal dynasty lost all semblance of power, and he never more remitted revenues to Delhi. Ali Verdi Khan ruled at Murshidabad for 16 years during a very troubled period. Throughout his time, the English settlements on the Hugli grew in power, which created the anxiety of the Nawab.

The Deputy Governors.—The three daughters of Ali Verdi Khan were married to their cousins the three sons of Haji Ahmad. To the eldest of his sons-in-law he gave the office of Deputy Governor of Dacca and to the youngest that of Orissa. He chose the son of the youngest Siraj-ud-Daula his successor.

Troubles of Ali Verdi Khan.—His first concern was to expel from Orissa the partizans of the late Nawab but this remote province was always the seat of difficulty and trouble in his after reign. In 1741 he was twice called away in person to take the field in Orissa.

Marhatta Invasion or Bargi raids.—While he was returning in triumph from Orissa on the second occasion, the Marhattas surprised him near Bardwan. This was the first time that these mounted marauders appeared in Bengal. They consisted of 40,000 cavalry and were sent by the chief of Berar to claim the *chauth* or the fourth part of the Bengal revenues. The Nawab's forces were quite unequal to cope with them. They lost all their baggage and after a running fight of three days, during which they endured the greatest hardships for want of food, reached Katwa and Ali Verdi Khan was safe. During the rainy season the Marhattas remained in the neighbourhood, plundering far and wide. The unfortunate inhabitants of Bengal suffered terribly from these pitiless and rapacious enemies, and the whole country was made desolate. Mir Habib who was an influential minister under the former Nawabs, joined the Marhattas and became a dangerous enemy of Ali Verdi Khan, At his instigation the Marhattas made an attempt upon the city of Murshidabad. They plundered the suburbs and are said to have obtained a booty of 3 *laks* of rupees from the bank of Jagat Seth. The inhabitants fled with their families to the other side of the Ganges and the Nawab despatched his treasures beyond Godagari.

The Marhatta Ditch and fortifications.—This was the time when the English obtained permission to fortify their territory. An entrenchment was dug at Calcutta, since known as the Marhatta Ditch. The factory at Kasimbazar was surrounded with a brick wall and bastians. In 1742 while the Marhattas were encamped at Katwa, Aliverdi Khan crossed the Bhagirati by a bridge of boats, attacked and defeated them. He gave them a second defeat at Midnapur.

Marhatta Invasion continued.—In 1743 the Marhattas returned in two separate bodies, one from Berar and the other from Puna. Aliverdi Khan himself avoided battle and contrived to engage one party against the other. By this means though he lost no men in the field, he paid an enormous sum to his Puna ally and the unhappy villagers were plundered indiscriminately by both the Marhatta parties. In the next year 1744, the Berar Marhattas again arrived and demanded the same contribution which their Puna brethern received the year previous. Ali Verdi Khan invited the leaders to a personal conference and caused them to be massacred. The Marhatta armies were next attacked and defeated. This preserved Bengal for two years from the Marhatta invasion. Behar and Orissa however became the scene of frequent revolts, battles and massacres.

Orissa ceded to the Marhattas.—At last in 1747, Ali Verdi Khan ceded to the Marhattas the province of Orissa and in addition agreed to pay them annually 12 laks of rupees as the *chauth* of Bengal. From this period till his death in 1756 Bengal was quiet.

Internal Rebellions.—During the Marhatta invasions Ali Verdi Khan was continually pressed by the rebellions of his own generals and near relatives. The first was that of Mastafa Khan, his own commander-in-chief. He succeeded in plundering Rajmahal and in seizing the fortress of Monghyr but was subsequently defeated and slain by Zain-ud-din, the Deputy Governor of Behar. The next rebellion was that of the Afghan troops, under Shamsher Khan. Zain-ud-din was slain by the rebels, and his aged father Haji Ahmad was tortured to death for not disclosing his treasures. The wife of Zain-ud-din, the daughter of the Nawab, and all his treasures fell into the hands of Shamsher Khan. Ali Verdi Khan set out against the rebels and met them at Barh near Patna. He utterly routed them, slew their leaders and rescued his daughter, 1749. The third was the unkindest blow of all. It was the rebellion of his grandson Siraj-ud-Daula, whom he had always treated with lavish kindness and whom long before he had nominated as his successor. The revolt was formidable but was promptly put down by the governor of Patna, Raja Janaki Ram.

Behar assessed.—In 1750 Ali Verdi Khan made a new assessment of the revenues of Behar. He divided it into 8 *sarkars* and 320 *mahals* and fixed the revenue at 95,56,098 rupees.

Death of Ali Verdi Khan.—Ali Verdi Khan died in his eightieth year, and was buried in the garden of Khush Bagh, on the right bank of the Bhagirati opposite Mati-jhil.

His character.—Ali Verdi Khan was never from his early youth addicted to idle pleasures. He was regular in his devotions, and was kind to his own relatives. Whether in his public or in his private duties he was always punctual. Mastafa Khan, his own general once tried to persuade him to expel the English from Calcutta and seize their wealth; but receiving no answer, he urged it again through the Nawab's nephews Nuazish Muhammad and Sayyid Ahmad. Ali Verdi Khan returned no answer, but shortly after said in private to the latter "My child, Mustafa Khan is a soldier, and wishes us to be constantly in need of his service, but how came you to join in his request? What have the English done against me, that I should use them ill? It is now difficult to extinguish fire on land; but should the sea be in flames, who can put it out? Never listen to such advice as his, for the result would probably be fatal."

The above expressions do not appear to be the outcome of his timidity, for in January 1749 a cause of quarrel arose between the English and the Nawab in which he exhibited his usual bold spirit. A king's ship had once seized several vessels, laden with goods of various Hugli merchants, Muhammadan and Armenian, and with things of great value belonging to the Nawab. Ali Verdi Khan sent a *purwana* to the Governor of Fort William, threatening that if he did not deliver all the merchants' goods and effects to them, he would give a due chastisement. He ordered *peons* on all the *gomasthas* of the Company's *arangs* and stopped the boats which were bringing down their goods. At Dacca he cut off the supply of provisions. He surrounded the factory of Kasimbazar with troops and compelled the English to his terms. The English got off by a payment of twelve *laks* of rupees. On another occasion, Ali Verdi Khan demanded the estate of a Turk, who died intestate at Calcutta. The Council forthwith paid up the value of the estate and were compelled to pay interest.

Siraj-ud-daula (1756—1757.)—His real name was Mirza Mahmud, but his grandfather procured for him from Delhi the title of Siraj-ud-Daula. In 1753, when he was only fifteen years old, his grandfather placed him by his side on the *masnad* as his successor. In August 1752 Siraj-ud-Daula arrived at Hugli. The Company's President and two other members of his council at Calcutta, went to greet him with a present worth Rs. 16,000. The President was received with the utmost politeness and distinction by the future Nawab, and the Court of Directors at home entertained large hopes of their future welfare.

His profligate character.—Immediately after his accession he proved to be profligate, vicious, oppressive, and in short of the vilest character imaginable.

His oppressions.—His uncle Nuazish Muhammad, who was governor of Dacca, died without any issue but leaving a very rich treasure. His widow Ghasiti Begum inherited the palace at Mati-jhil, where she lodged her treasures. The first act of Siraj-ud-Daula was to storm this palace and seize on the treasure of his aunt, which was worth 61 *laks* of rupees. He next dismissed his grandfather's old officers to make room for his young favourites. Among them was Mir Jafar who was *Bakshi* or Pay-master-general, and who since his dismissal commenced to plot against him. His next endeavour was to seize all the wealth of Raja Rajballav who was at first *peskar* of *Nawara* (naval fleet) and subsequently deputy governor of Dacca. A large portion of the money amassed by this man was conveyed out of his District by his son Krishna Das and taken into Fort

William. It was in search of this treasure that a quarrel arose between the Nawab and the English.

The first conspiracy against the Nawab.—Just at this time a conspiracy was formed by all those whom he had injured, to depose him and set up his cousin Saukat Jang. Mir Jafar Khan, after his disgrace, betook himself to the court of Saukat Jang at Purniah and urged him to seize the *masnad* of Bengal. In order to find out a pretext for the hostilities he was planning against Siraj-ud-Daula, Saukat Jang obtained from Gazi-ud-din, the Vazir of Alamgir II. Emperor of Delhi, a *firman* bestowing on him the *Subadari* of the lower provinces. These transactions came to the knowledge of Siraj-ud-Daula and he determined to attack Purniah. He advanced with an army as far as Rajmahal, when the complications with the English East India Company induced him to turn back and attack Calcutta.

Attack of Calcutta.—Two reasons are alleged for his taking up arms against the English :—(1) That the English had given refuge to Krishna Das, the enemy of the Nawab; and (2) that without any permission from the Nawab, they had established forts in the countries under his control. From Rajmahal the Nawab returned to Murshidabad, seized and plundered the Company's factory at Kasimbazar and took the English officers prisoners, amongst whom was Warren Hastings, then a youth of twenty-four. He then collected a powerful host, the command of which he gave to Ali Naki Khan and Ahmad-ul-Zaman Khan of Birbhum, along with Diwan Manik Chand, Bahar Mohan Lal, and Jafar Ali Khan. These marched against the English in the direction of

Calcutta, and encamped at Bagh Bazar, The English fled to Howrah, Bali and the fort. The women and children were sent on board a vessel, which weighed anchor and dropped down the river to Faltah. The Nawab attacked the fort, and carried it by storm.

The Black Hole.—The Nawab placed the English prisoners under the charge of Dewan Manik Chand, and returned to Murshidabad. The Dewan treated the captives with cruelty, and shut them up, one hundred and forty-six in all, in a small room 18 feet square with only two small windows barred with iron. It was only the English garrison prison in those days of cruel military discipline, known in history under the name of 'The Black Hole.' When on the next morning the door was opened, only 23 persons came out alive. This was in the year 1756.

Foundation of Alipur.—After this victory of the Nawab's, Ali Naki Khan took possession of a part of the enemy's country, and laid the foundation of Alipur, which is now the residence of the Lieutenant-Governor of Bengal.

Extortions from the Dutch and the French.—The Nawab on his way back from Calcutta to Murshidabad first extorted four and a half *laks* of rupees from the Dutch at Chinsurah, and then three and a half *laks* from the French at Chandarnagar, threatening to treat them in the same way as he had done the English.

Battle with Saukat Jang.—He next determined to test the allegiance of Saukat Jang, by appointing a Hindu courtier, named Ras Behari to the *Zemindari* of Birnagar. The Purniah Nawab resented the interference by publicly flogging the bearer of the message. Saukat

Jang then caused the Delhi *firman* to be openly proclaimed and bade Siraj-ud-Daula to withdraw from Murshidabad to any of the eastern districts. Siraj-ud-Daula immediately ordered his army to advance in two divisions. One, under his own command, marched up the right bank of the Ganges, while the other, under Raja Mohan Lal followed the left bank of the river. The Purniah army took its position behind a chain of deep morasses over which there was only one practicable causeway. The advantage of this position was sacrificed by the ignorant rashness of Saukat Jang. The Purniah cavalry was strong and was commanded by Hazari Lal; the artillery was weak and was in charge of Syam Sundar. The conflict that ensued took place at Baldiabari near Nawabganj. The cavalry of Saukat Jang was cut to pieces, and his artillery was silenced, and while Saukat Jang was advancing on an elephant; a musket-ball struck him on the forehead and killed him.

Recovery of Calcutta.—When the news of the disaster at Fort William in Bengal reached Madras, Clive and Watson promptly sailed to the mouth of the Ganges with all the troops that they could gather. Calcutta was recovered with little fighting. A peace was concluded with the Nawab. The Company were restored to all their privileges and their losses were made good. By the fourth article of the treaty, the Company were "allowed to fortify Calcutta in such manner as they might esteem proper"; and by the fifth, it was stipulated "that siccas be coined at Alinagar (Calcutta) in the same manner as at Murshidabad." This may be considered to have first established the Company's territorial character in Bengal.

Clive attacked Chandarnagar.—War had just then been declared between the English and the French in Europe. Clive captured the French settlement at Chandarnagar. Siraj-ud-Daula enraged at this, sided with the French.

Second conspiracy against the Nawab.—Meanwhile the Hindu subjects of the Nawab, disgusted with his violent and capricious behaviour, made a conspiracy against him, headed by Raja Raidurlab his treasurer. Mir Jafar who commanded 2,000 horse in the Nawab's service brought a proposal for betraying Murshidabad to the English with the help of the Seths. This proposal was conferred in secret with Mr. Watts, the resident at Kasimbazar. It was agreed that Mir Jafar should be set up as Nawab and the English should be richly rewarded and all their losses amply compensated. When the conspiracy was ripe, Umacharn (Omichand) who had been let into the secret, threatened to make a disclosure, unless his silence was purchased by a payment of thirty *laks*. Clive and the other conspirators were in despair. They then had a recourse to what is called the 'trick of the red treaty.' Two copies of the treaty were made out, one on white paper in which no mention of Umacharn's claim was made ; the other was on red paper in which all the money demanded by him was guaranteed. This piece of deception is a stain on Clive's character. Admiral Watson refused to sign the false treaty and Clive forged his name.

The Battle of Plassey.—Clive now with his usual bravery marched to the grove of Plassey, at the head of 1,000 Europeans and 2,000 sepoys with 8 pieces of artillery.

The Nawab's army numbered 35,000 foot and 15,000 horse with 50 cannon. Clive fought in spite of his council of war. The Nawab commenced the attack, while the English covered by a mango grove, remained on the defensive. The battle was languidly conducted, when Clive determined to make a vigorous assault. Mir Madan the Nawab's general-in-chief was slain and the whole army dispersed. The Nawab himself was seized with panic, mounted a swift camel and fled to Murshidabad, escorted by 2,000 of his chosen cavalry. This battle of Plassey was fought on the 23rd June, 1757.

Siraj-ud-Daula killed.—Siraj-ud-Daula fled in disguise from Murshidabad. His boat stopped at Rajmahal and he concealed himself in a deserted garden. Here he was detected by a Hindu whose ears he had formerly cut off and was betrayed to the troops sent in his pursuit. He was seized and taken to Murshidabad. Mir Jafar showed some compassion but his son Miran caused him to be put to death.

Share in Spoil.—Vast sums were paid to the Company and the losses of all merchants English, Armenian, and native were compensated. The army and the navy with their leaders, including Clive, Watson and the members of the council all shared in the spoil. Umacharn expected his thirty *laks* but was soon brought to his senses.

Maharaja Krishnachandra.—Maharaja Krishnachandra of Nadiya took a leading part in the establishment of the English. Lord Clive in recognition of his services conferred on him the title of Rajendra Bahadur.

Notes on the Mughal Rule.—Bengal was not divided into Districts during the Muhammadan rule. The only division of the country was in *Mahals*. *Sarkars* existed in the rent-roll of Todar Mall. But these were only revenue divisions, that is divisions for the purpose of collecting revenues. The words *subah* and *chaklah* belong entirely to the Mughal period.

Zemindars.—In ancient times Bengal was divided into a number of petty principalities, each ruled by its own prince. When the Muhammadans conquered the country, some of these princes were left in possession of their estates on condition of paying a certain revenue to the paramount power. Others were dispossessed. In the latter case government appointed its own officers, for the collection of revenue. The officers appointed to collect rents of large tracts of land, were called by Muhammadan rulers *Zemindars*, and the tract of land assigned was called *Zemindari*. The further subdivision of these tracts of land were called *parganas, tarafs, tapas* etc., over one or more of which *Zemindars* were placed. These *Zemindars* exercised a certain amount of police powers, levied tolls, duties and cesses. They had also power in matters of civil administration. As a rule these *Zemindars* paid their collections regularly. Abulfazl describes that "the people of Bengal are obedient and ready to pay taxes. They pay the taxes in eight instalments annually, in rupees and gold *mohurs*, which they bring personally to the treasury." Some of these *Zemindars* when they grew very powerful refused to pay revenue to the Bengal Governor. They were subjected to various sorts of persecutions and even in some cases military force was employed to bring them under control. We have seen the fate of Raja Protapaditya. Satragit, *Zemindar* of Bushna similarly rebelled and his rebellion ended as fatally for himself as the rebellion of Sitaram Rai, *Zemindar* of Mahmudpur.

Appointments.—We have seen that during the Mughal government, the Hindus were placed in such higher posts as the British government has not yet thought fit to offer. Raja Todar Mall and Raja Man Sing were appointed Subadars of Bengal; Jasawanta Rai was Dewan and Raja Rajballav was Deputy-Governor of Dacca. Alam Chand was Deputy Dewan of Bengal and was a member of the council of the Nawab. Raja Mohan Lal, Hazari Lal and Shyam Sundar each held the military post of general. Raja Rai Durlav was treasurer of Bengal. Raja Ram Narain was governor of Patna and Raja Ram Sing was governor of Midnapur.

The People.—Accurate informations are wanting as to the condition of the general people during the Mughal rule. There is no doubt however that they suffered oppressions from foreign invasions and sometimes at the hands of bad *Zemindars*. The cruelties perpetrated by the Afghan and Marhatta invaders were atrocious. At one time their name was a terror to the country and children were lulled to sleep with the name of the *Bargis*. In time of peace they enjoyed prosperity and their conditions were flourishing. Provisions were procurable at moderate prices. In the reigns of Shaista Khan and Shuja-ud-din rice sold at 8 or 10 *mans* for the rupee and in the time of Murshid Kuli Khan it sold at 4 *mans* for the rupee. At this time, the Muhammadan religion extended far and wide. It is known that at the time of Emperor Jahangir the Muhammadan religion extended in East Bengal up to the sea. From the census returns it is now seen that more than one-third of the population of Subah Bengal are Muhammadans. It is highly probable that the influence exercised by the Muhammadan *Zemindars* and *Jaigirdars* was the cause of so large a number of conversions to Musalmanism. Some consider that the non-aryans, when driven from the west, took refuge in the eastern districts, and in order to avoid their social degradation, embraced the religion of the governing race. Among the Hindus, the worship of *Vishnu* extended in all directions and the *Vaishnavas* constituted the great bulk of the community.

At that time the people had a local self-government of their own. The authority of the *Mandal* or village headman was undisputed. He decided disputes in his own village on boundary matters, caste questions, family disensions, &c. There was a village tribunal called *Panchayat* or committee of five selected by the people themselves from the gentry or the higher castes. They held their sittings for the punishment of offences, to settle disputes and to determine any local or social question. The tribunal had no legal binding authority but its decree was considered solemn and was generally respected in the village. The principal village officials were the *mal gamastha* appointed by the *Zemindar* to collect rents and grant receipts ; the *fauzdari gamastha* also a servant of the Zemindar, whose duties were to report offences to the police and to assist it in the investigation of criminal cases; the *choudris* whose business was to decide questions of price currents, fix rates of cart hire, &c. ; the *kanongoes* or village accountants; the *simandars* or *halshanas* who were charged with the protection of the village crops or boundaries; the *piyadas* who were entrusted with the watch and guard of roads. There were various other offices during the Mughal rule, the vestiges of which still survive in many proper names. These are—*Majumdars*, or treasurers; *sikdars*, subordinate revenue collectors; *mastangis*, examiners of accounts, ; *bakshis*, military paymasters; *hazaris*, or commanders of thousand men; *kotwals*, Muhammadan Police Magistrates; *khundakars* or valuers of crops, &c.

The most conspicuous persons in the village community were—*Purohits*, or priests; *Acharjya* or fortune-teller; *Napit* or barber; *Mahajan* or village usurer and grain merchant; *Kamar* or black-smith; *Chhutar* or carpenter; *Ful-mali* or gardener and preparer of garlands; *Dhoba* or village washerman.

Manufacture and trade.—The manufactures of Bengal were in a highly flourishing condition. The manufactured wares of this country attracted European traders as early as the sixteenth century. The fame of the fine muslins of Bengal, her rich silk and brocades, her harmonious cotton prints had spread far and wide in Asia, as well as Europe. The art of spinning and weaving afforded employment to a numerous population. Carpet-making, fine embroidery, jewellery, metal-work, saddlery, carving, paper-making, even architecture and sculpture developed to a considerable extent.

Education.—The Muhammadan government provided no means for the intellectual development of the people. The *Zemindars* however helped a great deal.

They established *patshalas* and *tols* for the benefit of the students of Sanskrit. They gave donations to distinguished pundits and provided *lakhraj* or rent free lands for the support of *chatuspatis*. In order that the learned Brahmans might cultivate their studies, they were relieved from the anxiety of earning a livelihood, by the grant of several *bighas* of *lakhraj* lands. A custom was also introduced of inviting and giving pecuniary presents to learned Brahmans on occasions of *sradhas*, marriages, &c. Among the literary personages who flourished under the patronage of the Nadiya Raja were Ramprasad Sen, a Sanskrit scholar; Bhumesvar Vidhyalankar, an eminent poet; Saran Tarkalankar, a Naiyaik or logician; and Anukula Bachaspati, a great astronomer. The Naiyaik Kalidas Sidhwanta was the presiding pundit of the Court of the Maharaja Krishna Chandra. Bharat Chandra was one of the ornaments of his Court. *Kabikankan* Mukunda Ram Chakravarti flourished under the patronage of the Mednipur *Zemindar* Bankura Rai and his son Raghu Nath Rai.

Language and Literature.—During the latter part of the Mughal rule, the cultivation of the Bengali language was set on foot. The first Bengali poem was *Chandi* written by Kabikankan. It was followed by the *Ramayan* of Krittibas, the *Mahabharat* of Kasi Das and the *Padabali* of Ramprasad. Bharat Chandra was the first who improved and ennobled the Bengali language. His *Annada Mangal* and its episode *Vidya-Sundar* is remarkable for the richness of its language and felicity of illustration. Bharat Chandra at first found great difficulty in embodying his ideas in Bengali. He found the language inadequate in expressions. But he obviated these difficulties by the introduction of Sanskrit words. The Bengali language, however, was formed during this period by rendering it the medium of poetical compositions only.

Culture of Religion.—From the beginning the Brahmans have guided the bulk of the Hindu population in all religious matters. They have been themselves considered as divine and their instructions have always been accepted as authoritative. When there was no proper language and literature of the country, a system of religious teaching was introduced, in which a learned Brahman interpreted the holy *shastras* to an assembly consisting of the lower and the less educated classes, in his own language and in the most impressive way. These interpreters are designated *kathaks*. By their exertions the Bengali language was first commenced to be formed. There is no doubt that the earliest Bengali poets Krittibas and Kasidas wrote their Ramayan and Mahabharat by hearing the interpretations of these *kathaks*. Hence these works differ from the original texts in Sanskrit.

The use of Spirits.—Dr. Rajendra Lal Mittra has shown conclusively by a profusion of instances taken from Sanskrit literature, ancient and mediæval, that spirits and other intoxicating drinks have been extensively used in India at all times and by all classes. Their use was condemned by moralists and lawgivers but rice-spirit was used in sacrifices in the earliest Vedic times. The *Tantras* afford the most indubitable proofs of a strong attachment on the part of a large section of the Hindus to over-indulgence in spirituous liquors. They were, however, never made a source of revenue in Hindu India and were never taxed.

We find in a list of taxes in the *Ain Akbari*, that both salt and spirituous liquors are mentioned to have been taxed under the Mughal Emperors. In the accounts of the revenues of Bengal, as settled by the Nawab Jaffir Khan in 1722 A.D., and confirmed by his successor Sujah Khan, seven years afterwards, the taxes on spirituous liquors are treated in two ways. In some parts of the country they were realized by the *Zemindars* and then consolidated with the *mal* in the total assessment. In other parts they were collected by temporary officers of government. It is probable that there was an unrestricted system of out-stills existing at the time and the price of spirit was less. But the social, moral, and religious influences put a sufficient check upon the increase of drunkenness. Complaints were then rife about the spread of drunkenness among the lower classes of the people.

CHAPTER X.

THE COMPANY'S NAWABS OF BENGAL.

Mir Jafar (1757—1760).—On the 29th June, 1757, six days after the battle of Plassey, Colonel Clive entered the city of Murshidabad, escorted by a guard of 200 Europeans and 300 *sipahis* and took possession of the palace and garden of Morad Bagh, which had been allotted as his residence. On the same day he visited the Nawab's palace at Mansurganj and took Mir Jafar by the hand into the hall of audience, led him to the empty *musnad* of Siraj-ud-Daula and seated him thereon. Clive himself presented before him a plate containing gold *mohurs* and congratulated him on his accession as Nawab of Bengal, Behar and Orissa.

Treasures of the late Nawab.—Difficulties soon arose about the payment of the price of this elevation. Colonel Clive, Mr Watts, Mr. Lushington, Ramchand the writer, and Naba Krishna the *munshi* entered the vaults of the palace. They found stored up there Rs. 17,60,000 in silver, Rs. 23,00,000 in gold, two chests of ingots, four chests of set jewels, and two smaller ones containing loose stones and gems. It is supposed that there was an inner treasury of Siraj-ud-Daula which contained eight *krors* of rupees, and the whole of which was distributed by Mir Jafar, Ramchand, Naba Krishna, and Amin Beg Khan among themselves. This is not incredible. Ramchand at the time of the battle of Plassey was a writer on Rs. 60 a month. He died ten years afterwards, worth Rs. 72,00,000 in cash; and he left 400 large water pots, 80 containing gold and the rest silver; Rs. 18,00,000 in land, and jewels to the value of Rs. 20,00,000. The wealth of Naba Krishna can be judged from the fact that he spent nine *laks* of rupees in the funeral obsequies of his mother. As political *banian* to the Company his salary, in 1767 was Rs. 200 a month.

The Company claimed ten millions of rupees for its losses and large sums were also demanded for the English, Hindu and Armenian inhabitants of

Calcutta. The Members of the Council received large sums.

Zemindari of Calcutta.—On the 20th December 1757, a tract of country containing about 882 square miles, known as the '*Zemindari* of Calcutta' or the '24 Parganas *Zemindari*' was ceded by Mir Jafar to the East India Company.

Jaigir Sanad granted to Lord Clive.—Mir Jafar gave the Company the jurisdiction of a land-holder; but on the 13th July, 1759, the Delhi Emperor granted for it a *Jaigir sanad* to Lord Clive for services rendered by him in aiding in the suppression of a rebellion headed by the Emperor's eldest son, Shah Alam. Thus Clive became the landlord of his own masters, and received from the Emperor the title of *Shash-hasari, Panj hasar Sawar*, or commander of Six thousand (personal) and Five thousand Horse.

The First Governor.—In 1758, the Court of Directors appointed Clive, as the first Governor of all the Company's Settlements in Bengal.

Abdication of Mir Jafar.—Mir Jafar became extremely extravagant in his expenditure and could not overcome his financial embarrassments. The energy of his son Miran supported the Government for a season but he died in 1760. The troops, who were left unpaid for a long time, broke into open revolt and Mir Jafar was compelled to cede his power to the more capable hands of his son-in-law Mir Kasem.

Mir Kasem (1760—1763.)—Mir Kasem won the *musnad* by distributing among the members of Council 20 *laks* of rupees, as the price of his elevation. At the same time he assigned to the Company the revenues of the three Districts of Bardwan, Mednipur, and Chittagong.

His able administration.—Mir Kasem restored order to the administration and reduced to obedience all rebel *Zemindars*. He introduced reforms, which enabled him within eighteen months to clear off his dues to the English and to satisfy the arrear pay of troops. He reorganised his army on the model of the Company's *sipahis*. He removed his capital to Monghyr and began to meditate driving the English out of Bengal. His favourite general Gurghin or Gregory Khan, once an Armenian cloth merchant of Ispahan, established an arsenal in the fort.

Rupture with the English.—The rupture with the English soon arose and the immediate cause was, that the Company's servants claimed an absolute freedom from transit duties in all departments of their trade. Whenever the Nawab's officers interfered they were punished. Mr. Vansittart, a Madras civilian was now the governor of Fort William, and the chief of the Company's Factory at Patna was Mr. Ellis a very headstrong man. Mir Kasem agreed to the settlement of the duty payable by the English traders to be 9 per cent. a rate which was immensely below that exacted from other traders. This also was disagreeable to the Company's servants. A deputation consisting of Mr. Hay and Mr. Amyatt were despatched to Monghyr. But it was too late for negotiations.

Bengal reconquered by the English.—Disputes between the *Gamashtas* of the English and the Nawab's officers broke out in every district. Mr. Ellis occupied the city of Patna with his *sipahis*. The Nawab in revenge seized under the walls of Monghyr some boats with arms, while they were passing up the Ganges to Patna. Mr. Amyatt, while returning to Calcutta was attacked by men of the Nawab near Kasimbazar and massacred. The war opened favorably for the Nawab. The English at Patna were attacked, overpowered and taken prisoners. The whole of Bengal as far as the present District of Nadiya was occupied by the Muhammadans and the factory of Kasimbazar was for the second time plundered. The English collected their forces at Agradwip near Nadiya. After some petty engagements, the English recovered possession of Murshidabad. The Nawab was defeated in two pitched battles by Major Adams, at Gheria on the 2nd August and at Udha-nala on the 5th September, 1763. The English obtained a complete victory, and Bengal was for the second time conquered.

Mir Kasem's cruelty.—Mir Kasem fled to Monghyr, where exasperated by the defeat he caused the two Seths Mahtab Rai Jagat Seth and Maharaja Swarup Chand, and the late Deputy Governor of Dacca Raja Raj Ballav to be thrown from a high tower into the Ganges. He also killed Ram Narayan a former governor of Patna. They were murdered on suspicion of their favouring the English. Shortly after this, the members of the council Mr. Ellis, Mr. Hay and Mr. Lushington with 100 soldiers were shot at Patna by Samru, a German or rather Swiss, whose original name was Walter Reinhard, the general of the Nawab. It is said that 200 Englishmen were killed at this time throughout Bengal.

Patna recovered.—A *lak* of rupees was offered for the person of Mir Kasem and Rs. 40,000 for Samru. They took the protection of the Wazir of Oudh who refused to surrender them. Shah Alam, who had now succeeded his father as the Emperor of Delhi and Shuja-ud-Daula, Wazir of Oudh, united their forces and threatened Patna, but the English recovered it after a vigorous fight.

First Sepoy Mutiny.—At this time, the *first* sepoy mutiny took place in the Bengal army. This was quelled by Major (afterwards Sir Hector) Munro, who ordered 24 of the ring-leaders to be blown from guns.

Battle of Buxar.—In 1764 Major Munro led his army against the Wazir and won the decisive battle of Buxar. It made the English supreme in Hindustan. The Emperor himself came to the English camp and opened negotiations with the Calcutta Council for his restoration.

End of Mir Kasem.—After the battle of Buxar, Mir Kasem took refuge among the Rohillas; finally he retired to Delhi, where he died in 1777 in great indigence and obscurity.

Mir Jafar (1763-1765.)—On the first outbreak of hostilities, the English resolved to depose Mir Kasem and set up another Nawab. Negotiations were opened with Mir Jafar who was now residing at Calcutta for his own safety. He was now willing to consent to every demand and was accordingly installed a second time at Murshidabad. The price of his elevation was more than one lak and seventy thousand rupees. Besides, the Company's servants gained their main object, the exemption of their own goods from all duties. Mir Jafar was already broken by age and disease and he died in January, 1765.

Nazim-ud-Daula (1765-1766.)—The English chose the eldest surviving son of Mir Jafar to succeed his father. The Members of the Council received from him fourteen *laks* of rupees, which they divided among themselves. The new Nawab was about 20 years of age and died within three years. But during his short rule, the English power was first established in Bengal, to rule in future the destiny of whole India.

First English Governor of Bengal.—In May, 1765, Lord Clive arrived at Calcutta with full power as *Commander-in-chief, President* and *Governor* of Bengal. Within two months, he proceeded to Murshidabad. The Nawab was compelled to give up the management of the revenue and the command of the troops into the hands of the English. An annual sum of *sikka* Rs. 53,86,131 was allowed to him for the expenses of his Court and the administration of justice. He was further placed under the control of a Board of advisers, consisting of Raja Durlabh Ram, Jagat Seth and Muhammad Reza Khan. An Agent was also kept at Murshidabad for general superintendence. The character and power of the new Nawab can be well imagined, when after the settlement of the above proposals, he exclaimed "Thank God, I shall now have as many dancing girls as I like." The total income of Bengal with its dependencies was, in 1765, about 3 *krors* and 32 *laks* of *sicca* rupees.

Grant of Dewani to the Company.—Lord Clive next proceeded to the English camp in the northwest, and there received personally from the Emperor Shah

Alam, the grant in perpetuity of the Dewani or financial administration of Bengal, Behar and Orissa, * on the 12th August, 1765.

First Punya Ceremony.—In the following year Lord Clive took his seat as Dewan at Mati-Jhil, in concert with the Nawab, who sat as Nazim and opened the *punya* or the ceremony of the first collection of the annual revenue, in full *darbar*. On the 8th May, 1766 a few days after this ceremony Nawab Nazim-ud-Daula died.

Saif-ud-Daula (1766—1769.)—The brother of the late Nawab, Saif-ud-Daula, a youth of sixteen succeeded him. By the treaty with the Company which placed him on the *musnad*, he consented to accept a fixed annual stipend of *sikka* Rs. 41,86,131 for the maintenance of himself and his household. He died of small-pox in 1769. This was the year of the great famine, still known in Bengal as the famine, of the year seventy-six, for it happened in the Bengali year 1176. The calamity caused the death of about a third of its population.

Organization of the Company's Service.—In the year 1767, the next year after the *punya* ceremony, Clive devoted himself to the re-organization of the service. As the salaries which the Company gave to their servants† were inadequate, they were allowed to

---

* The Orissa of this period included only the District of Mednipur and a part of Hugli, or more accurately the tract of country lying between the rivers Subarnarekha and Rupnarain. Orissa proper was conquered and annexed from the Marhattas by Lord Wellesly in 1803.

† At this time there was a resident at the Nawab's court who inspected the management of the Naib Dewan, and a

receive presents and to engage in private trades. Clive disallowed these, but at the same time to enable the servants of the Company to live decently, he established a society for conducting a traffic in salt, the profits of which were to be divided among them, according to their rank. This arrangement continued for two years, when a commission of 2½ per cent. was substituted in its stead. He next introduced reforms in the army. He abolished the double *batta*, which the English forces were receiving from the time of Mir Jafar. The result of this was a mutiny. But Clive put it down in the course of a fortnight with an iron hand. He marched up to Monghyr and Benares, arrested the ring-leaders and ordered them to be tried by a Court Martial. The others, on making due submission, were forgiven.

Retirement of Lord Clive.—As the health of Clive was now seriously affected, he left the shores of India for ever on the 16th of January, 1767. He was received in England with every mark of respect and greatness. But his enemies, out of envy, tried to put him to dishonor and shame. He had repeatedly to explain and defend his various acts in Parliament but the House at length came to the resolution that he had rendered great and meritorious services to his country.

---

chief who superintended the collections of the province of Behar, under the immediate management of a distinguished native, Sitab Rai. But with these exceptions, there were no other covenanted servants of the Company in the interior, except those who were administering the *Zemindari* lands of Calcutta and the 24-Parganas, and the ceded districts of Bardwan, Mednipur, and Chittagong.

Though thus honorably acquitted, under the pressure of mental and bodily sufferings he committed suicide in November, 1774, by taking large doses of laudanum.

The second Governor.—Clive was succeeded in the Government by Mr. Verelst, a man of strict honesty but without a fixedness of purpose. The servants of the Company, who had been obliged by Clive to sign the Covenants, again plunged into the trade of the country and the management of the revenue fell into disorder.

Mubarak-ud-Daula (1769-1796.)—After the death of Saif-ud-daula, his minor brother Mubarak-ud-Daula, a child of but a few years of age, was appointed Nawab. The Governor and Council of Fort William agreed to pay him an annual stipend of *sikka* Rs. 31,81,991. In the year 1771, the Court of Directors in England, resolved on a new policy. They had determined to 'stand forth as Dewan, and by the agency of the Company's servants to take upon themselves the entire care and management of revenues.' The infancy of the Nawab helped them to carry out their policy. On the plea of his non-age the annual stipend of the Nawab was reduced to sixteen laks of rupees. The reduction was effected in January, 1772.

Warren Hastings.—On the 13th of April of the same year, Warren Hastings arrived at Calcutta as Governor. Clive had laid the territorial foundations of the British Empire in Bengal, Hastings created a British administration for that empire. The reforms he effected will be treated in the next chapter. By them, almost all the functions of government were transferred directly into English hands. The superintendence of the administration of Criminal Justice was left in the hands of the Muhammadans during the rule of Warren Hastings, which again was taken in the hands of the English in the time of Lord Cornwallis.

The Supremacy of the Company.—From this time, Lord Macaulay says "the heir of Mir Jafar still resides at Murshidabad, the ancient capital of his house, still bears the title of Nawab, is still accosted by the English as 'Your Highness,' and is still suffered to retain a portion of the regal state which surrounded his ancestors. A pension of one hundred and sixty thousand pounds a year is annually paid to him by the Government. His carriage is surrounded by guards, each preceded by attendants with silver maces. His person and dwelling are exempted from the ordinary authority of the ministers of justice. But he has not the smallest share of political power, and is in fact only a noble and wealthy subject."

Titular Nawabs-Nazim.—The Nawab Mubarak-ud-Daula died in 1796. His successors Nazim-ul-mulk (1796), Saizad Zain-ud-din Ali Khan (1810), Humayun Jah (1821), and Mansur Ali Khan (1838) simply bore the title of 'Nawab Nazim.'

The Nawab Bahadur of Murshidabad.—The title was in 1883 taken away and the present Nawab Ali Kadr, the head of the Murshidabad Nizamat family, was installed on the 27th March 'The Nawab Bahadur of Murshidabad.'

CHAPTER XI.

THE COMPANY BAHADUR'S RULE IN BENGAL.
SECTION I.
The Administration of Governors-General.

Warren Hastings, (1772—1785.)—The plan of double government between the Nawab and the Company proved a failure. Before the year 1793, there was no organised or established system of the Company's administration. The collection of the land revenue formed the chief, if not the only, administrative business. There was no revenue officer in Bengal, and the native Zemindars were left to oppress the ryots and defraud the Company. In 1769 European supervisors were appointed by Mr. Hastings, who proved no better than the former. In this state of profound disorder, seven years elapsed since the acquisition of the *Dewani* by the Company.

In 1772 the Court of Directors resolved to "stand forth as Dewan, and by the agency of the Company's servants, to take upon themselves the entire care and management of the revenues." The plan, then adopted by Mr. Hastings and the four members of his council for the internal government, was as follows :—

Revenue Department.—At the Presidency, a Committee of Revenue was appointed, consisting of Mr. Hastings as President and a Council of four Members, with an Accountant-General and assistants and a native functionary, who was termed Rai Rayan. The offices of Naib Dewan, of Murshidabad and of Patna, were abolished; and the treasury was removed from Murshidabad to Calcutta. In respect to the provinces, it was resolved that the Supervisors should be designated Collectors, with each of whom a native officer styled Dewan was joined, in the superintendence of the revenues.

Judicial Department.—Two courts were instituted for each provincial division or collectorship,—"one by the name of *Diwani* or Civil court, for the cognizance of civil causes; the other named *Fauzdari* or Criminal Court, for the trial of crimes and misdemeanours."

The Collector presided over the Civil Court, attended by the provincial native Dewan and other officers. In the Criminal Court, the *Kazi* and *Mufti* of the district and two *Maulvis*, sat to expound the Muhammadan law, and to determine how far criminals were guilty; but it was the Collector's duty to supervise their proceedings, and satisfy himself that the decision passed was fair and impartial. The Collector had no further concern in the criminal administration.

Appeals from these Courts were allowed to two superior Courts, established at the chief seat of government,—one under the denomination of *Sadar Diwani Adalat* or Chief Court of Civil Judicature; the other the *Sadar Nisamat Adalat*, or Chief Court of Criminal Justice.

The *Sadar Diwani Adalat* consisted of the President and Members of Council, assisted by native officers. In the *Sadar Nisamat Adalat*, a chief officer of Justice presided, appointed by the Nazim, and assisted by the head

Kazi and *Mufti* and three eminent *Maulvis*. Over this latter Court, a control was vested in the President and Council, similar to what was exercised by the Collectors in the provinces. But it was soon found, that the superintendence over criminal justice, when exercised by the President, involved too heavy duties; and in October, 1775 the Court of *Nizamat Adalat* was moved back to Murshidabad, and again placed under the control of the well known Muhammad Reza Khan, who was appointed Naib Nazim.

Revenue Settlement.—Mr. Hastings sent out the four members of the committee, to go throughout the land and effect a revenue settlement with the land-holders for five years. During this land settlement, the *Zemindars*, it is said, suffered a great deal of oppression, at the hands of corrupt native underlings and rapacious English officers. Ganga Gobinda Singh, the founder of the family of the Rajas of Kandi, was Dewan of Warren Hastings, and he amassed an immense fortune at this time. It is said that he spent twenty *laks* of rupees, during his mother's *sraddha* ceremony.

The Regulating Act.—In 1773 an Act of Parliament was passed, called the Regulating Act. It came into operation in 1774. Its chief provisions were :—that the Directors were to be elected for four years; that the Governor of Bengal should henceforth be the Governor-General, who should be assisted by four councillors; and that the other British possessions in India were to be subordinate to Bengal; and that a Supreme Court of Judicature was to be established at Calcutta.

The First Governor-General.—From 1772 to 1774,

Mr. Hastings was Governor of Bengal, and from the latter date to 1785, he was the Governor-General of India.

Early Forms of Administration.—In 1774, the European Collectors were recalled from the provinces, and native *amils* were appointed in their stead. A new plan of police was introduced. Native officers styled *Fausdars* were appointed to the fourteen districts or local jurisdictions, into which Bengal was now divided. The superintendence of the collection of the revenue, removed from the Collectors, was vested in six Provincial Councils, which were established at Calcutta, Bardwan, Dacca, Murshidabad, Dinajpur, and Patna.

The administration of civil justice was, on the same principle, transferred to the *amils*.

The Members of the Council.—The new Members of the Council, and the Judges of the Supreme Court, landed in Calcutta on the 19th October, 1774. The first Members of the Council were Mr. (afterwards Sir Philip) Francis, Colonel Monson, General Clavering and Mr. Barwell. They were all prejudiced against Mr. Hastings. They considered him as an incarnation of injustice and as they formed the majority in the Council, they successfully opposed him in all measures. Mr. Barwell alone supported him.

Charges against Mr. Hastings.—At the instigation of Mr. Francis and his associates, charges of bribery and embezzlement were preferred against the Governor-General, but they were not substantiated. He was accused, of having received a share of the amount embezzled by Mr. Graham, whom he had appointed guardian of the person and property of the minor son of

Tilak Chandra, *Zemindar* of Bardwan ; and was also accused, of appropriating a portion of the allowance which the native *Fauzdar* of Hugli continued to receive, even after the administration of the Company had commenced. A more important charge was brought by Nanda Kumar, who accused Mr. Hastings of having received a bribe of 3½ *laks*, on the occasion of the appointment of Mani Begum and his son Raja Gurudas to the management of Nawab's household at Murshidabad. But the charge was not brought home against him.

Charge against Nanda Kumar.—Mr. Hastings now preferred a charge in the Supreme Court against Nanda Kumar, for a conspiracy to criminate him. The judges kept Nanda Kumar on bail.

The trial of Maharaja Nanda Kumar.—Soon after Nanda Kumar was arrested on a charge of forgery, at the suit of a native merchant named Mohan Prosad. He was brought to trial, found guilty and sentenced by the Chief Justice Sir Elijah Impey to be hanged in 1775. Nanda Kumar was a Brahman, and therefore his execution created a great sensation ; and Mr. Hastings was suspected of having unjustly procured it. Though he was afterwards formally acquitted of the charge, the event has cast upon him a shade of suspicion, not likely to be soon effaced.

Judicial Reform of 1780.—When the Supreme Court was instituted, its power was not well-defined, and the judges interfered with every department of the state. They issued writs against the Zemindars on the oath of any person, dragged them to Calcutta, and if they could not give bail threw them into prison. The authority of the *Zemindars* was subverted, and the collection of revenue ceased, and the ryots withheld their rents. In April 1780, Mr. Hastings remodelled the judicial establishment of the country. In each of the six great provincial divisions of the country, a court of justice distinct from, and independent of the Revenue Council, was established. Over this court, a covenanted servant presided, whose jurisdiction extended over all civil and rent cases. These six divisions were, in their civil aspect, augmented shortly to eighteen, to remove the inconvenience of extensive jurisdiction. The Judges of these courts were wholly unconnected with the Revenue Department, except in four frontier districts of Chittra (or Hazaribag), Bhagalpur, Islamabad (or Chittagong), and Rangpur, where the offices of Judge, Magistrate, and Collector, were vested in the same person.

Simultaneously with the extension of the Civil Courts, the Provincial Councils were abolished, and Collectorships reinstituted (1781). All the revenue affairs of the provinces were brought down gradually to the Presidency, there to be administered by five of the most able and experienced of the civil servants, under the designation of a "Committee of Revenue."

The establishment of *Fausdars* and *Thanadars*, introduced in 1774, was abolished in 1781, and the eighteen civil judges were vested with the powers of a Magistrate. But as Magistrate they merely exercised the powers of an executive police. They had powers of apprehending *dakaits* and criminals, but the trial and the infliction of punishment were left to the native Muhammadan officials. Provision was at the same time made for cases, where with special permission of the Governor-General and Council, *Zemindars* might be invested with such part of the police jurisdiction, as they formerly exercised under the ancient Mughal Government.

The Supreme Court.—The Supreme Court, which was an entirely separate institution, was governed by English law and administered by three Judges, Barristers-at-Law, appointed by the Crown, of whom the chief was styled 'Chief Justice.' It had full jurisdiction in Calcutta and also a personal jurisdiction over all persons in the employment of the Company, including *Zemindars*, revenue farmers and contractors in the Muffasil. This extensive power led to confusion and injustice; and a new Act was passed in 1781, defining and limiting the powers of the Crown Court. The jurisdiction of the Supreme Court was confined, to the limits of the City of Calcutta between the Hugli and the Marhatta ditch, and to the determination of all serious cases, in which European British subjects were accused and committed for trial. It was strictly prohibited by law from interfering in matters of revenue.

Second Land Revenue Settlement.—The plan, which Mr. Hastings had devised in 1772 for collecting the land revenue, proved a failure. The *Zemindars* generally contracted for more than they were able to pay, while the ryots were impoverished by oppressive exactions. The term of the first settlement expired in 1777, and the Directors ordered that the lands should be let out for one year only, on the most advantageous terms, but not by auction.

Bengali Types—Under the patronage of Mr. Hastings,

Mr. Halhed, a civilian of eminent talents, prepared from native works a code of Hindu and Muhammadan laws which was printed in 1775. In 1778 he published the first grammar of the Bengali language, which was printed at Hugli, for as yet there was no press in the metropolis. Mr. Charles Wilkins with his own hands cut and cast the first fount of Bengali types, which had ever been seen, and with them Mr. Halhed's Grammar was published (1778).

The first newspaper.—On the 29th January, 1780, the first newspaper published in India, made its appearance at Calcutta.

The Calcutta Madrasha.—In 1781 the Madrasha or Muhammadan College of Calcutta was founded.

The Asiatic Society of Calcutta.—In the year 1783, Sir William Jones came out to this country as one of the judges of the Supreme Court. He was one of the most illustrious Englishmen who have ever appeared in Bengal. He did material good to the country. In the year 1784, he established the 'Asiatic Society of Calcutta,' for the cultivation and study of Oriental languages and literature.

Pitt's India Bill.—In the year 1784, Pitt introduced his famous bill in Parliament, and brought forward a plan for the better government of India which was carried out and continued in force till the year 1858, when it was directly transferred to the Crown. So long the affairs of the East India Company had been conducted by a Court of Directors, and checked by a General Court of Proprietors of India Stock. A Board of Control was formed, which was to consist of six members of the

Privy Council, chosen by the king, who were to check and control all that might be done in the India House. They had the power of appointing the Governor-General.

Impeachment of Mr. Hastings.—In February 1785, Hastings left India, after an eventful administration of 13 years. Twenty-two charges were brought against him in the House of Lords by Burke, of cruelty and oppression to the natives of India. The trial commenced in the Westminister Hall on the 13th of February, 1788, and was dragged out to the wearisome length of 7 years; but at last he was declared not guilty upon every charge.

Kanta Babu and Devi Singh.—Of the two other natives, who brought him disrepute, were Kanta Poddar and Devi Singh who made large fortunes during his rule. Kanta Poddar or Kanta Babu as he was generally called, was the founder of the Kasimbazar Raj family, now headed by the illustrious Maharani Sarnamayi. Devi Singh was a very unprincipled man. His cruelties towards the poor ryots of Dinajpur cannot be read without a feeling of horror.

The Early Company's Police.—During the early part of the English administration, the Police of the Company's Government was quite unable to maintain order, and the whole country became a nest of robbers and *dakaits*. As an illustration we may mention the story of Biswanath Babu. He was a *bagdi* by caste, and was an inhabitant of Asanagar 10 miles from Krishnagar. The gang under him numbered 500 dakaits. He exercised his vocation in broad day-light, sending previous notices to those whom he intended to plunder. He attacked the factory of Mr. Samuel Fady, an indigo planter of Nadiya. He was subdued with great difficulty, by the aid of a few European sailors under Mr. Blacquiere. Biswanath and a dozen of his accomplices were tried, convicted and capitally sentenced. They were hanged on a scaffold on the river side. Their corpses were caged and suspended from a *Bat-tree* for public exhibition and as a warning to evil-doers. To put down gang robbery, the Company was obliged to pass the severest laws. They ordered that the *dakait* should be executed in his own village; that his family should become the state slaves; and that the whole village should be fined, each individual according to his means.

The Pahariahs.—Of the European officers who did good to the country, at this time, may be mentioned the name of Mr. Augustus Cleveland, who was then Collector of Bhagulpur. The Paharias, who lived to the south of the place, frequently committed raids upon the plains and plundered the cultivators. The terror they occasioned so overspread, that the alluvial country was deserted by its cultivators, and no boat dared to moor after dusk on the southern bank of the Ganges. Cleveland, by his exertions and mild policy, soon changed the face of the country, and the Paharias were brought into peaceful habits. The landholders of the District have erected a monument of brick to the memory of Mr. Cleveland. A monument of stone was sent by the Court of Directors from England, and has been placed in front of the house which Cleveland occupied.

Character of Warren Hastings.—The character of Warren Hastings may be summed up in the following words of an eminent statesman;—" though he was not blameless, if there was a bald place on his head, it ought to be covered with laurels."

Sir John Macpherson.—Mr. Hastings was succeeded in the government by Mr. (afterwards Sir John) Macpherson, the late agent of the Nawab of Arcot. His administration of 20 months was judicious and he effected great improvements in the management of the finances.

Lord Cornwallis (1786—1793.)—Lord Cornwallis twice held the high post of Governor-General. His first rule is celebrated for :—(1) the introduction of the Permanent Settlement into Bengal, (2) the judicial reforms.

The Permanent Settlement.—The chief glory of Lord Cornwallis' administration, consists in the revenue and judicial reforms, which he effected. Lord Cornwallis regarded the body of the *Zemindars* as the proper aristocracy of Bengal. With a view to promote the future ease and happiness of the people, and to effect improvements in agriculture, he declared them to be lawful owners of the soil, and made a settlement with them at first for ten years, generally known as the decennial settlement. He promised that the settlement should be permanent, if it should prove satisfactory. At last in 1793, their tenure was declared to be a permanent transferable interest in the land, to be held at a fixed revenue under government for ever. The police and other powers, which the Zemindars exercised during the Muhammadan administration, were either modified or taken away entirely. Their duties were eventually laid down by an enactment as follow :—

(1) That *Zemindars* should not in future exercise

any judicial or police powers, but should merely assist the constituted police in the prevention and discovery of offences.

(2) That they should give information of the occurrence of heinous offences to the police, and of designs to commit the same.

(3) That they should bear the expense of providing *dak* establishment, for the conveyance of letters from police station to police station, and from police officers to Magistrates.

(4) That they should contribute to the construction and maintenance of roads and maintain embankments.

(5) That they should not collect any tax or internal duties.

(6) That they should neither do, nor allow to be done, acts prejudicial to the public revenue.

(7) That they should provide supplies at current *bazar* prices to troops on march and afford facilities for crossing rivers.

Tracts comprised in the Permanent Settlement.—The permanent settlement thus effected, embraced roughly speaking, the tracts of country now comprised in the divisions of Bardwan, the Presidency, Rajshahi, Dacca, Chittagong, Patna, and Bhagalpur. It also comprised parts of the Hazaribag and Manbhum districts in the Chutiá Nágpur division, as well as Jalpaigari, Goalpara and Kuch Behar.

Judicial Reforms.—Under instructions which Lord Cornwallis brought with him from England in 1786, the revenue and judicial institutions of the country were again modified.

The Committee of Revenue changed its designation to that of 'Board of Revenue.' The European Civil servants, superintending the several districts into which the country was divided, were each of them vested with the united powers of Collector, Civil Judge and Magistrate. It was only in the administration of justice in the cities of Murshidabad, Dacca, and Patna, that district courts were established, superintended by a Judge and Magistrate.

Administration of Criminal Justice.—The administration of criminal justice remained, however, vested in the Naib Nazim as before. But towards the end of 1790, a very important change took place in this arrangement. It was declared that with a view "to ensure a prompt and impartial administration of the criminal law, and in order that all ranks of people might enjoy security of person and property, the Governor-General in Council resolved to accept superintendence of the administration of criminal justice throughout the provinces." The *Nizamat Adalat* or Chief Criminal Court of Justice, was again removed from Murshidabad to Calcutta, to consist of the Governor-General and Members of Council, assisted by the head native law officers.

Courts of Circuit.—Four Courts of Circuit, superintended respectively by covenanted servants of the company, each with their Muhammadan law officers, were in 1793 established for the trial of cases not punishable by the Magistrates.

Separation of Judicial and Financial Powers.—In 1793 the financial and judicial powers were again separated. A new court of Civil Judicature was established in every district. The new Judge was vested with the powers of Magistrate as well as of Civil Judge. This arrangement long continued, one officer in each district being Judge and Magistrate, and another Collector. To the Courts of Justice, a Registrar and one or more assistants were appointed. The Assistants were Assistants to the Judge and Magistrate. The Registrar was empowered to try civil causes not exceeding 200 rupees.

Appointment of Native Commissioners.—At the same time, a regulation was enacted authorising the appointment of native Commissioners to hear and decide, in the first instance, on suits of personal property not exceeding the value of Rs 50. These were of three descriptions, *viz.*, *Amins* or referees; *Salisans* or arbitrators, and *Munsifs* or native justices. The referees and arbitrators were usually *kasis*, appointed by virtue of their offices; the *munsifs* were more carefully selected. They were not paid by fixed salary, but by commission on the amount of causes investigated by them. Appeals from their decisions lay to the Civil Judge.

Provincial Courts of Appeal.—In order to ensure the hearing of appeals from the judge, which had previously lain direct to the Governor-General at Calcutta, Lord Cornwallis established by Regulation V of 1793, four provincial courts of Appeal* at Calcutta, Murshidabad,

---

* The territorial jurisdictions of these Courts were as follows:—
(1) *Calcutta Division*—24 Parganas, Bardwan, Jungle Mahals, Mednipur, Cuttack, Jessore, Nadiya, Hugli, Foreign settlements of Chinsura, Chandarnagar and Serampur.
(2) *Murshidabad Division*—Murshidabad, Bhagulpur, Purniah, Dinajpur, Rangpur, Rajshahi, Birbhum.

Dacca and Patna. Each Court was superintended by three Covenanted Civilian Judges, and to which a Registrar and one or more Covenanted Assistants were attached. An appeal lay from them to the *Sadar Diwani Adalat* or Governor-General and Council in Calcutta, when the suit exceeded Rs 5,000 in extent. These Civil Courts were identical with the Courts of Circuit. The same officers, European and native, were attached to the Courts in their Civil and Criminal jurisdictions.

Increase of pay of officers.—The real measure of effectual reform, was to increase the pay of every officer of government, so that he might not be induced to acquire money by corrupt practices.

Departure of Lord Cornwallis.—Lord Cornwallis left India in October, 1793 after a most successful administration.

Sir John Shore (1793—1798.)—Lord Cornwallis was succeeded by Sir John Shore (afterwards Lord Teignmouth), a member of the civil service, who greatly distinguished himself in carrying out the measures of the Permanent Settlement, though he had been an opponent of it in principle. His five years' administration was uneventful.

Marquis of Wellesley (1798—1805.)—Lord Mornington, afterwards the Marquis of Wellesley, reached Calcutta on the 18th May, 1798. His career was the most brilliant period of the Indian history. During his time, the empire extended to one-third beyond its former size, and

---

(3) *Dacca Division*—Dacca, Maimansing, Syhlet, Tipperah, Chittagong, Bakarganj, Dacca Jellalpur.
(4) *Patna Division*—Patna, Ramghar, Behar, Tirhut, Saran, Shahabad.

the revenue increased to fifteen *krors*, forty *laks* of rupees.

The Missionaries.—In October, 1799, the first Protestant Missionary establishment was formed at Serampur by Dr. Marshman and Mr. Ward and their colleagues. Dr. Carey who had come six years before, joined them. These missionaries were the pioneers of Indian civilization. They improved the Bengali language, and published the *Mahabharat*, the *Ramayan* and many other works in Bengali. They first established Bengali schools in the country.

The College of Fort William.—In order to instruct the young members of the Civil Service in the language and literature of the country, Lord Wellesley established the College of Fort William in Calcutta, in the year 1800. On their arrival in India, they were placed in this institution, and it was not until they had passed an examination, and were reported qualified for service, that they were provided with appointments. Various works in Bengali and other oriental languages were compiled and printed for the use of this institution. The Bengali books, compiled were *Pratapaditya Charit* (1801), and *Lipimala* (1802) by Ram Ram Basu, *Krishna Chandra Charit* (1802) by Rajib Lochan, *Rajabali* by Mrityunjai Vidyalankar an Uriya, and Bengali grammar and dictionary by Dr. Carey.

Sacrifice of Children at Gangasagar.—Lord Wellesley on the 20th August, 1802, prohibited the custom for parents to sacrifice their children at Gangasagar. He sent a company of *sipahis* to prevent it. Though this measure was a direct interference with the religious prejudices of the people, it gave general satisfaction and not a word of complaint was uttered by any class of people.

Annexation of Orissa.—In 1803, after the war with the Bhonsla Raja of Nagpur, the whole of Orissa was forfeited by him to the English. Thus forty-eight years after it had been ceded to the Marhattas in the last year of Ali Verdi's reign, Orissa was re-annexed to Bengal.* The temple of Jaggannath was taken under the protection of the British troops. The priests were left to manage the affairs of the temple and to collect and expend the tax. Three years after, however, the English government to increase its revenue took charge of the temple, and collected the tax through its own officers. A portion of the revenue was devoted to the temple, the balance went to the public treasury.

Rebellion of Kharda Raja.—Soon after the annexation of the province, towards the close of 1804, the Raja of Kharda revolted. He had hopes that the Company's government would restore to him the *parganas*, which the Marhattas had wrung from him. But the English decided to retain them, as they had been taken from the Marhattas, who were in actual possession of them at the time of the conquest. The Raja was disappointed, and in October the disorderly mob of *paiks* and peons of the Raja made a raid on the villages in the vicinity of Pippli, and carried off all the cattle and other moveable property. Troops were sent from Ganjam, and the rebels were quickly driven out of Pippli, who retreated to the fort at

---

* See foot note page 118.

Kharda. The fort was stormed, and the Raja made good his escape southwards. A few days after he surrendered, and was placed under close confinement in the fort of Cuttack. His territory was confiscated.

The Sadar Court.—Lord Wellesley found that the Governor-General and members of council, could not properly discharge the duties of the *Sadar Nizamat Adalat*; he therefore abolished it as well as the *Sadar Dewani Adalat*, and established the 'Sadar Court.' He placed it in the hands of three judges, giving them jurisdiction in all civil and criminal matters. This Sadar Court remained as the final court of appeal till 1862. The Sadar Court was latterly composed of five or six covenanted civilians, more or less, as might be necessary.

Departure of Lord Wellesley.—Lord Wellesley left for England towards the close of 1805.

Marquis of Cornwallis again (1805.)—This time Lord Cornwallis came with instructions to bring about peace at any price. He landed in Calcutta on the 30th July, 1805. He proceeded without delay to north-west, but being an old man and broken in health, died on the 5th of October of the same year at Gazipur.

Sir George Barlow (1805—1807).—Being the Senior Member of the Council, Sir George Barlow succeeded as Governor-General. He literally carried out the commands of his employers, and curtailed the area of the British Territory.

The Pilgrim tax of Jaggannath.—It was during the administration of this Governor-General, that the government received the pilgrim tax of Jaggannath, and assumed the direction of the temple. This system continued for more than thirty years The Raja of Kharda was released in 1807 and allowed to reside in Puri.

Lord Minto (1807—1813).—On the 31st of July, 1807, Lord Minto arrived at Calcutta. During his administration the transit duties were increased, the effect of which was that trade was interrupted, and the people suffered a good deal.

Superintendent of Police.—A superintendent of Police was first appointed under Regulation X. (1808) for the divisions of Calcutta, Dacca, and Murshidabad, and under Regulation VIII. (1810) similar arrangement was made for Patna.

Renewal of the Company's Charter.—In the year 1813, the twenty year's term of the Charter of the Company, granted before by Parliament expired. A new Charter was given with very important changes. So long the trade between England and India remained exclusively in the hands of the Company. "But the Company which had begun with a counting house, was now seated on the throne of India." Trade was therefore opened to the merchants, and the Government was retained in the hands of the Company.

Preaching of the Gospel.—Missionaries were permitted to preach the Gospel and a Bishop was appointed for Calcutta and one Archdeacon for each of the towns of Bombay and Madras.

Education of the people.—The education of the people received the attention of Government, and annually a *lak* of Rupees, from the public revenue, was ordered to be spent for this purpose.

Lord Moira (1813—1823).—On the 4th of October,

1813, Lord Minto resigned the Government of India in the hands of Lord Moira, better known by his title Marquis of Hastings. His long rule of nine years was marked by the campaign against the Gurkhas of Nepal and the last Marhatta War.

Division of Districts into Thanahs.—For the purposes of revenue administration, the country had been divided by the Mughal government into *parganahs*, each *parganah* comprising a certain number of villages. But this arrangement fell into such decay, that in some districts the *parganah* boundaries could hardly be ascertained. By Regulation XXII. of 1813 more compact arrangements for purposes of police were adopted. Magistrates were directed to divide their districts into police jurisdictions, to be named after the places at which the chief police officers were stationed. And in this way the term *Thanah* which originally meant only the police station, came to be applied to the jurisdiction subordinate to that station. Large *Thanahs* were divided again into outposts or *Phanris*.

Second Kharda insurrection.—In the year 1817-18, the second Kharda insurrection burst with such sudden fury, as to threaten the expulsion of the English, if not from the whole of Orissa, at least from the territory of Kharda. It was headed by a brave and clever Uriya named Jagabandhu. The resumption of a large tract of service land, the payment of land-tax in silver instead of in *cowries*, the heavy salt duty, the extortions of Bengali officials, were all bitter grounds of discontent. Jagabandhu himself at the head of a disorderly band of *paiks*, captured the town of Puri, and burnt the Government Court-house and several other public and private buildings. Puri was therefore abandoned. Martial law was extended to the towns and neighbourhood of Puri and Pippli. An officer who had been despatched with a force, found all quiet there. He proceeded to Kharda and came upon the rebels, who fled in the wildest dismay and confusion, as soon as fire was opened. The force resumed its march on Puri, entered the town, and captured the Raja who was on the point of taking flight. He was taken to Calcutta and placed in confinement in Fort William, where he died in November, 1818.

First Outbreak of Cholera.—On the 20th August, 1817, it was at Jessore that the first outbreak of cholera began, which, spreading across the valley of the Ganges, extended itself in a north-westerly direction over the civilized world. Cholera had been known before as an endemic disease, prevailing more or less in almost every part of Lower Bengal, but previous to 1817 it had not that dreadful form which is now associated with the name. Within two months from its first outbreak, ten thousand people are stated to have died in the District. On the 15th September the epidemic appeared in Calcutta, and about the same date in Bardwan, whence it started on its fatal journey northward.

Education of the people.—Lord Hastings had the enlarged view of raising the people in the scale of civilization, though some regarded their ignorance as a security for the continuance of the British supremacy. A new era now commenced in the history of Bengal. Schools were set up, and the first Bengali newspaper was published on the 29th May, 1818, under the title of *Samachar Darpan*. About the same time the Calcutta School Book Society was established, through the efforts of Dr. Carey and Mr. Bayley. Large schools were established by the Missionaries at Chinsurah and Serampur. The Hindu College was also established through the exertions of Sir Edward Hyde East, Mr. Harington and Mr. David Hare. The last named man was a great philanthropist and at one time his name was known to every household of Bengal.

Two other Bengali Newspapers.—Two other Bengali newspapers were published in 1820 and 1821. The one was *Sangbad Kaumadi*, published under the patronage of Raja Rammohan Rai, and the other was *Samachar Chandrika*.

Board of Revenue for the Lower Provinces.—Lord Cornwallis changed the name of the 'Committee of Revenue' of Mr. Hastings to that of the 'Board of Revenue.' In 1795 the province of Benares was added to the Company's dominions and laws were published for the newly acquired province of Benares. In 1807 a Commission was constituted, consisting of two members for the superintendence of the settlement of these provinces, and for the general control of the Collectors in the discharge of their several public duties. These Commissioners were vested with all the authority that had hitherto been exercised by the Board of Revenue of Calcutta. In 1809 this Board of Commissioners was declared permanent; and at the same all the powers, that up to this period had been exercised by the Calcutta Sadar Board of Revenue in the province of Benares, were transferred to the Board of Commissioners. In 1816 a separate Commissioner was appointed for the superintendence of the revenues of the province of Benares, and that part of the province of Behar which was comprised in the Zillas of Behar, Shahabad, Saran, and Trihut, and he was vested with all the authority, that had previously been exercised in these provinces by the Board of Revenue and Board of Commissioners respectively. In 1817 the authority of the Behar-Benares Commissioner extended to the districts of Ramghar, Bhagalpur and Purniah. In the same year, two Commissioners were appointed in the place of the single officer, and accordingly the Board of Commissioners in Behar and Benares was established. As a special case, the general revenues of Dinajpur and Rangpur were also entrusted to this Board. In 1819 the management of the revenues of Dinajpur and Rangpur were replaced under the Calcutta Board of Revenue. In 1822 considerable changes were effected in these arrangements. The districts of Bhagalpur and Purniah were replaced under the Calcutta Board of Revenue, which continued to exercise its powers in the districts subordinate to its authority, and which was henceforth denominated the 'Board of Revenue for the Lower Provinces.' Two other Boards of Revenue were established, namely, the 'Board of Revenue for the Central Provinces,' and the 'Board of Revenue for the Western Provinces.'

Departure of Lord Hastings—Lord Hastings left India in January, 1823, after a brilliant rule of nine years. He extended the territories of the Company, increased the revenues, reduced debt, and left the treasury full.

Lord Amherst (1823—1828.)—Between the departure of Lord Hastings and the arrival of Lord Amherst, Mr. Adam acted as Governor-General. His rule was remarkable only for the odious measure of laying restrictions on the Press.

Lord Amherst's Rule.—Lord Amherst's administraton of five years, is known for the first Burmese war and the capture of Bharatpore.

The Sanskrit College.—In the year 1824, through the efforts of Professor Wilson, the Sanskrit College of Calcutta was established.

Assam put under the Government of Bengal.—After the annexation of Assam and Kachar by the treaty of 1826, the Commissioner of the North-East Frontier was styled the Commissioner of Assam, and put under the Government of Bengal.

English the paramount power in India.—In 1827, Lord Amherst proceeded to the west and visited Delhi. In his conversation with the king, he distinctly expressed that whatever vassalage, the English owed to the Mughal Government, was at an end ; that the English were now the paramount power in India.

Departure of Lord Amherst—Lord Amherst retired in March 1828.

Lord William Bentinck (1828-1835.)—Twenty years before Lord William Bentinck was Governor of Madras. On the 4th July, 1828, he arrived at Calcutta as Governor-General. His rule was one of administrative reform and of improvement to the people. From his time people could understand that the British rule in India was providential, and was intended for their happiness. The character of his rule is well described in the inscription upon his statue in Calcutta. "He abolished cruel rites; he effaced humiliating distinctions; he gave liberty to the expressions of public opinion; his constant study was to elevate the intellectual and moral character of the nations committed to his charge".

His Internal Administration.—His first attention was directed to reduce the public expenditure. He appointed two Commissions, one for the examination of the civil and the other of the military accounts. Notwithstanding all the clamour that was raised against the reduction, he succeeded in making a permanent reduction of 1½ *krors* of rupees from the expenditure. He reduced his own pay from 3 to 2½ *laks* a year.

The Abolition of Sati.—His two most memorable acts, were the abolition of *Sati* and the suppression of the *Thags*. The custom of widows, burning on their dead husbands' funeral-pile, had long been practised in India and acquired the sanctity of a religious rite. Lord Bentinck determined to abolish it. Against the strenuous opposition both from Europeans and Natives, on the 4th December, 1829, he extinguished this cruel and murderous practice, by declaring—"that any one who should abet the commission of *Sati*, should be guilty of culpable homicide." The influential natives who supported this benevolent act, were Raja Ram Mohan Rai, Dwarka Nath Tagore and Rai Kalinath Choudhuri.

The Suppression of the Thags.—The *Thags* were a band of assassins who allured travellers to their snare, and murdered them by strangulation. They travelled in gangs, disguised as merchants or pilgrims, and carried on their profession without mercy. The honor of suppressing them is due to Captain (afterward Sir William) Sleeman and his coadjutors. Between 1826 and 1835 no less than 1,562 *thags* were apprehended.

The Revenue and Judicial Changes.—Under Lord William Bentinck, extensive changes were again effected in the Judicial, Revenue and Police systems. By regulation I. of 1829 the executive officers of both police and revenue, were placed under the superintendence of Commissioners of Revenue and Circuit, each of whom was vested with the charge of four or five districts. Lord W. Bentinck abolished the Provincial Courts, and the Commissioners were appointed to go on circuit as Sessions Judges. The appointment of Superintendent of Police was abolished, and vested in the Commissioner with the fullest Police control. The Revenue Boards in the *provinces* were also abolished, and their powers vested in the Commissioners under the control of the *Sadar* Board at Calcutta. Thus the Commissioners were absolutely to superintend both the finance and the criminal justice of their different divisions. But these arrangements were not found completely successful; and after a few years, in 1831 the judicial powers of the Commissioners were transferred to the Civil Judges.

The Judges, under Lord William Bentinck, held a jail delivery every month. But the Judges were also the Magistrates, and so they were unable to cope with their additional duties. They were therefore divested of their magisterial responsibilities, and these were transferred to the Collector. This was the creation of the present unit of the administration, the Magistrate and Collector, or the executive head of each district. Under Regulation VIII of 1833, the appointment of Additional Judges was sanctioned.

The Young Bengal.—Now came a period of transition in Bengal. As a result of the English education, a revolution commenced to take place in the social, moral and religious organization of the country. The young educated men of the time despised Hinduism, and looked down on the caste-system. Their habits and opinions and even their mode of life changed. In attempting to imitate the English, they imitated more their vices than their virtues. The old Hindu feelings of attachment, obedience, reverance for age could no longer hold their sway, and a social disorder was the consequence.

The Brahmo Samaj of Calcutta.—At this crisis, Raja Ram Mohan Rai well undersanding that social and moral order can only rest on a religious basis, established in the year 1829 the Brahmo Samaj of Calcutta. He adopted Theism, and endeavoured to give permanence and vitality to the old Hindu scriptures, the Vedas.

The Bengali Literature.—Raja Ram Mohan Rai was a profound scholar, and he contributed largely to the improvement of the Bengali language, by writing many Bengali works. It was he, who first gave a form to the Bengali prose. The famous Iswar Chandra Gupta commenced to publish his *Pravakar* in 1830.

Titu Miyan's Insurrection.—At this time occurred what is known as Titu Miyan's insurrection. This man made a pilgrimage to Mecca, where he met Sayyid Ahmad, the founder of the Indian Wahabi Sect. Titu, the leader of the *farajis*, had ordered his followers to wear beards of a certain length, and the Hindu landlords imposed a tax of 5 *sikis* (R. 1. 4 as.) on each Muhammadan tenant who should wear such a beard. This is said to be the immediate cause of their outbreak. They commenced a series of agrarian outrages, and the whole of the country, north and east of Calcutta, including the 24 Parganahs, Nadiya and Faridpur, lay at their mercy. They plundered villages, burnt mosques and defiled Hindu temples by slaughtering cows. They proclaimed that the English rule was extinct, and Muhammadan power re-established. On the 23rd October, 1831, the insurgents selected the village of Narikelberia, in the 24 Parganahs, for their head quarters, and erected a strong bamboo stockade around it. A detachment of the Calcutta Militia was sent out on the 14th November against the rebels, but the soldiers were cut to pieces. Regular troops were then sent against the insurgents. After a stubborn engagement, they were driven back and their bamboo fort was taken by storm. Titu Miyan fell in action. Of the survivors, one was condemned to death and one hundred and forty were sentenced by the Court to various terms of imprisonment.

Native Judgeships.—In 1831, Lord William Bentinck established a higher grade of native Judgeships. Previously to this period, there had been but two classes of native Judges, with very limited powers. The higher class was known as *Sadar Amins*, the lower as *Munsifs*. Lord Cornwallis denominated the *munsifs* as commissioners. In 1803, the office of *Sadar Amin* had been instituted, with a jurisdiction extending to suits of Rs. 100.

In 1821 the *munsifs* had been empowered to try cases extending to Rs. 150, whilst the *Sadar Amin* took cognizance of cases to the amount of Rs. 500. In 1827 the authority of the latter had been doubled. Lord Bentinck now established a superior class of judicial officers, known as Principal Sadar Amins, with enlarged powers and higher salaries. They were subsequently authorised to try cases involving property to any amount, and an appeal lay from them to European Judges.

Appointment of Deputy Collectors.—The office of uncovenanted Deputy Collector was established under Regulation IX of 1833. The appointment was, in the first instance, open only to "natives of India of any class or religious persuasion," but was extended by Act X. of 1843 to all persons of whatever religion, place of birth, descent, or colour. This class of officers was found useful and their powers were by degrees enlarged, and their numbers increased, and they were employed in all branches of the administration.

Annexation of Cachar.—In 1824 the Burmese had invaded Cachar. The Raja sought the assistance of the British, who expelled the Burmese and replaced him on the throne in 1826. In 1830 the Raja died without issue, and under the terms of the Treaty, Cachar lapsed to the British Government. In August 1832, the district was placed under the Agent to the Governor General in Assam. It was transferred to the Dacca division in 1833.

Renewal of the Company's Charter.—In the year 1833, the Charter of the East India Company was renewed for twenty years with great changes. The Company was obliged to give up all connection with the trade in India, and to sell their factories. A Legislative Council was formed at Calcutta, to consist of all the ordinary members and of a law member. A law commission was also nominated, to frame a code of laws for the whole country. Lord Macaulay was the first legal member of the council, and first President of the Law Commission.

Governor-General as Governor of Bengal.—Up to 1834, the whole of the Bengal Presidency, including Benares and the ceded and conquered provinces of upper India, were directly administered by the Governor-General of Bengal in Council. In 1834 the Governor-General in Council became Governor-General of India, and Bengal was then governed by the Governor-General, in the capacity of Governor of Bengal without a Council. From this time the civil history of Bengal, Behar, and Orissa, became entirely separate from that of the upper Provinces.

Chutia Nagpur Agency formed.—After the suppression of the Kol insurrection in 1831-32, the South-western Frontier Agency of Chutiá Nágpur was called into existence by Regulation XIII. of 1833.

Commencement of English Education.—During the administration of Lord William Bentinck, great encouragement was given to the education of the people. Opinions differed whether the education to be imparted, should be in Sanskrit or in English. Lord William Bentinck was of opinion, that the study of the English language would prove highly beneficial. From this time commenced the diffusion of English education in this country.

The Medical College of Calcutta.—The Medical College of Calcutta was established in 1835. It is now the largest medical school in the world.

Other Improvements.—In order to promote economy among the people, Lord Bentinck established a Savings Bank in Calcutta. A monthly steam communication, between India and England by the *overland route*, was established, though the Directors threw every obstacle in the way.

Close of His Rule.—Lord William Bentinck's able administration closed in March, 1835.

Lord Metcalfe (1835-1836.)—Sir Charles (afterwards Lord) Metcalfe succeeded Lord William Bentinck, as Governor-General, being the senior member of Council. His short rule is memorable for giving entire liberty to the Press. This measure was initiated during the administration of his predecessor; he carried it into execution, though the Court of Directors expressed a strong apprehension, that the concession of this privilege would imperil the very existence of their Government.

The Company's Coin.—On the 1st September, 1835, the Company's Rupee weighing 180 grains, consisting of 165 grain of pure silver and 15 grains of alloy, was ordered to be coined. It was declared to be equivalent to the Bombay, Madras, Farakkabad and Surat Rupees, and to fifteen-sixteenths of the Calcutta Sicca Rupee, which ceased to be a legal tender in 1836. It was also declared at this time, that no gold coin should henceforth be a legal tender of payment in India.

Lord Auckland (1836-1842.)—Lord Auckland arrived at Calcutta on the 4th of March, 1836. His rule is famous for the annihilation of the British troops in Afghanistan, in attempting to place Shah Shuja upon the throne of Kabul.

Muhammad Mashin's Fund.—In 1814, a wealthy Muhammedan gentleman, named Muhammad Mashin, owning a fourth share of the great Sayyidpur estate in the district of Jessore, died without heirs, leaving his estate valued at Rs. 45,000 a year, for pious uses. The great Imambara or Mosque of Hugli is maintained out of this fund. In 1836, this fund was devoted in founding and endowing the Hugli College.

Dacca College.—In 1835 an English Seminary was first established by Government at Dacca. Two years later, it was reported to be in a flourishing condition. In 1841 the school was raised to the position of a College, and the foundation stone of the present building was laid.

Darjiling Sanitarium.—A part of the hill portion of the district of Darjiling, was ceded by the Raja of Sikim in 1838, and in acknowledgement of the cession, an annual subsidy of Rs. 6000 was granted to the Raja. Darjiling was created a sanitarium.

Annexation of Assam.—In 1833 upper Assam was granted to Raja Purandar Sing as a tributary, and similar engagements were entered into with the chiefs of several other tribes. Gradually the whole of the country was brought under the British administration, and in 1837 a code of rules for the administration of Assam, was drawn up by the Sadar Court with the sanction of Government.

Administrative Changes.—The union of the offices of Magistrate and Collector, as established under Lord

William Bentinck, was only of temporary duration. In 1837, Lord Auckland and the Court of Directors sanctioned the separation of the offices of Magistrate and Collector.

Superintendent of Police.—Under Act XXIV. of 1837 the Government was again empowered to appoint a Superintendent of Police, and in such case the Commissioner was to cease to exercise any powers in regard to the Magistracy and Police. In Bengal a single Superintendent of Police was accordingly appointed.

Abolition of the Pilgrim-tax of Jaggannath.— In 1840 the Company abolished the pilgrim tax of Jaggannath, and made over the entire management of the temple to the Rajas of Kharda. It was considered, that the money received from the pilgrim tax was to a certain extent the price of a state sanction to idolatry, and by the abolition of the tax, the Company removed this stain from its administration.

Lord Ellenborough (1842-1844.)—Lord Ellenborough arrived at Calcutta on the 21st February, 1842. During his administration the avenging expedition into Afghanistan under General Pollock was undertaken. Kabul was conquered, its inhabitants were punished, the prisoners were recovered and then the country was evacuated. The country of Sindh was conquered and annexed to the British territory. In 1844 he was recalled by the Court of Directors.

Appointment of Deputy Magistrates.—In 1843 an Act was framed, empowering the government to appoint in any district one or more uncovenanted Deputy

Magistrates, with or without Police powers as might be determined.

The Tatwabodhini Patrika.—In the same year the *Tatwabodhini Patrika* commenced to be published, and Babu Akshay Kumar Datta became its editor. The Bengali language was found inadequate for the expression of subtle and nice distinctions, and the difficulty was removed by the admixture of Sanskrit words. Next to Raja Ram Mohan Rai, Babu Akshay Kumar Datta and Pundit Isvar Chandra Vidyasagar are the two great writers to whom Bengali prose owes its formation. It would also be worth while to mention that at this time, the *kabiwallas*, *jatrawallas* and the *punchaliwalas* helped unnoticed in the development of Bengali language.

Lord Hardinge (1845-1848.)—Sir Henry (afterwards Lord) Hardinge next succeeded as Governor-General. He had served in the Peninsular War, and had lost one hand in the battle of Waterloo. The first Sikh War was the chief event in his rule.

Administrative Changes.—The progress of separation of the office of Magistrate and Collector, sanctioned by Lord Auckland, went on gradually until 1845. In that year the magisterial and fiscal officers were disunited everywhere, except in three districts of Orissa and in the independent Joint-Magistracies of Pabna, Maldah, Bogra, Bhulluah, (or Noakhali), Faridpur, Bankura, Barasat, and Champaran.

Social Improvements.—Lord Hardinge encouraged free trade, and sanctioned the establishment of one hundred vernacular schools in different parts of Bengal.

The Krishnagar College.—The Krishnagar College

and the Government English school attached to it, were established in 1846.

Betal Panchavinsati.—In 1847 Pandit Isvar Chandra Vidyasagar published his *Betal-Panchavinsati*.

Earl of Dalhousie (1848-1856.)—Lord Dalhousie arrived at Calcutta on the 12th January, 1848. His rule is marked by large acquisitions of territory, and for considerable improvements tending to the material prosperity of the country.

Annexations of territory.—His campaigns, in the Panjab and Burmah, ended in the complete annexation of the former, and a partial annexation of the latter to the British dominion. Nagpur, Oudh, Jhansi, Berar and several minor states also came under British rule.

His internal Reforms.—No branch of the administration escaped his reforming hand. He founded the Public Works Department; he opened the Ganges Canal; and he promoted the steam communication with England by the overland route. The Postal Department was matured and cheap postage was introduced by him. The Railway and Telegraph lines were first started during his administration.* The Educational Department received his closest attention, and on the system inaugurated during his rule, the education of India still rests. The Barhampur College was established in 1853, and the Presidency College in Calcutta in 1855. The Calcutta University was ordered to be founded. Many Model vernacular Schools were established. The system of female education was inaugurated, and the Calcutta

---

* The railways began in India in 1850 and the first train ran on the 18th November, 1852.

Bethune School was founded in 1848. The old Education Committee was abolished, and the posts of Director of Public Instruction and Inspectors of Schools were created, and the system of grant-in aid of schools was devised.

Literary Improvements.—The *Vividartha Sangraha* or Bengali penny magazine was commenced in 1851, by the Vernacular Literature Society. The *Krishi-Sangraha* was the organ of the Agri-Horticultural Society. The *Arunodai* was conducted by the Christian Tract Society. The *Bharatbarshiya Sabha Bijnyapani* was the organ of the British Indian Association.

Drinking of the People.—During the first half of this century, 'drinking' increased among the people. On moral grounds, the tax on spirituous liquors was resumed in 1790, (see p. 111). The excise of liquor has in Bengal been conducted, under three general systems;—the *farming*, the *daily* or *monthly tax* also called the *outstill* and the *sadar distillery*.

The farming system.—Under this system, the excise revenue—sometimes of a district, sometimes of part of a district—is farmed out on tenders invited and selected. The farmer works outstills by his own servants, or underfarms the right as regarded each outstill.

The daily tax or outstill system.—The Collector decides where shops for the retail sale of country liquor are required. He then puts up to auction, for the ensuing year, the right to set up a still at the place indicated, and to open a shop in connection with such still. The bidder of the highest amount of daily or monthly tax gets the right.

The sadar distillery system.—Certain central distillery buildings are erected by Government; and at these any number of distillers, the building can accommodate, are allowed to set up stills. The liquor distilled is tested, and they pay duty according to its strength. The liquor is sold by the distiller to shopkeepers, who pay a license fee for leave to keep open a retail shop.

The daily tax was the system first in force. In 1813 the farming system and the sadar distillery system were both partially introduced. In 1824 the farming system was greatly extended. The farmer had but one object—private gain; and the more shops be opened, and the greater the consumption of liquor, the better was this object attained. Thus drunkenness became more common, than it had been previous to the introduction of the British system of administering the excise department. The primary cause, however, of the growth of the habit of drinking among the people was due to the people themselves. The restrictions which had previously kept large classes from indulging in spirituous liquors, were relaxed by the social, moral and religious changes effected during the English administration.

Renewal of the Company's Charter.—In 1853 the charter of the East India Company was renewed. Among many other changes, it was ordered that Bengal should be put under a Lieutenant-Governor. So long Bengal remained under the Governor-General as Governor, his place during his occasional absence being supplied by a Deputy Governor appointed from among the members of his Council.

Lieutenant Governor of Bengal.—On the 12th October, 1853, the Court of Directors authorised the

COMPANY'S RULE.

appointment of a Lieutenant Governor of Bengal, and the Hon'ble F. G. Halliday was the first Lieutenant Governor appointed.

Departure of Lord Dalhousie.—Lord Dalhousie left Calcutta on the 6th March, 1856, after a vigorous and brilliant reign which lasted eight years.

SECTION II.
The Administration of Lieutenant Governor.

Sir Frederick Halliday (1854—1859.)—Sir Frederick Halliday's rule in Bengal falls under two Governors-General, Lord Dalhousie and Lord Canning, partly under the East India Company and partly under the British Crown.

Jurisdiction of the Lieutenant Governor.—The jurisdiction of the Lieutenant Governor was declared to be co-extensive with that of the former Governor of Bengal, with the exception of the newly annexed Burmese provinces, which remained under the direct authority of the Government of India.

Trade Route of East Bengal.—In 1853 a scheme for the improvement of the Sundarban * navigation, between Calcutta and East Bengal, was devised; and though it proved unsuccessful, gradually a very important trade route was formed and great facilities were offered for the passage of boats.

---

* The derivation of the word *Sundarban* is uncertain. According to some it is *Sundari* 'Sundari tree' and *ban* 'forests,' the whole meaning 'the Sundari forest.' According to others it is Sans. *Samudra* or Urdu *Samundar*, 'the sea,' and *ban* 'forest,' the whole meaning the 'forest near the sea.'

The Hindu Patriot.—In 1853 the English newspaper 'Hindu Patriot' was started by Babu Haris Chandra Mookerjea. It was he who taught the natives to discuss political subjects. Since his death many newspapers in English and Bengali have been published conducted by Bengali Editors but only three or four are equal, if not superior to the Hindu Patriot.

Superintendent of Police abolished.—On the 23rd March, 1854, the Court of Directors sanctioned the abolition of the appointment of the Superintendent of Police, and the transfer of his duties to the respective Revenue Commissioners.

The Santal Parganahs.—The enquiry into the causes of the Santal insurrection in 1855 brought to light, that the tracts of country now designated the Santal Parganahs were unsuitable to the regulation system, and were accordingly exempted from the operation of the general regulations. The excepted tract was placed under the Commissioner of the Bhagalpur Division, assisted by a Deputy Commissioner and Assistants and Extra Assistant Commissioners.

Dealing with the Bhutan Government.—The people and Government of Bhutan, in 1856 and subsequently, carried off several of the British subjects from the tract which is situated on the west bank of the Tista within the district of Rangpur. This tract had been given up to the Bhutians in 1779 by the orders of Mr. Hastings, from a desire to avoid all misunderstanding with the Bhutan Government. In 1842 it again came into British possession subject to a yearly rental of 2,000 Rupees. This annual payment was stopped, as the

Bhutan Government did not release the prisoners carried away by them.

The Calcutta University.—The Calcutta University was constituted by an Act of the Legislature in 1857. The preamble of the Act recited, that the University was established "for the better encouragement of Her Majesty's subjects in the pursuit of a regular and liberal course of education." The Calcutta University has no professors or scholars or Colleges and Schools: its function is to examine and confer degrees.

The Sepoy Mutiny.—The principal event during the rule of this Lieutenant-Governor was the Sepoy Mutiny. It broke out in northern India and spread down into Lower Bengal. The places where the revolt made its appearance in Bengal Proper are Barhampur, Barrackpur, Chittagong and Dacca.

Barhampur.—Early in the year 1857, the excitement about the new greased cartridges was felt in every cantonment. At Barhampur there were no European troops; a regiment of native infantry the 19th was stationed there. They heard the report of the greased cartridges and were panic-struck. On the night of the 27th February, they were ordered for parade the next morning. They thought they would be forced to use the obnoxious cartridges, seized upon the bells of arms and broke out in tumult. An explanation was given to them and they were pacified. On the next morning they appeared in the parade ground penitent and humble. But it was thought that their offence should not be over-looked, and so they were ordered to Barrackpur to be disbanded.

Barrackpur.—There were then four Native Infantry

regiments at Barrackpur—the 2nd Grenadiers, the 43rd, the 34th, and the 70th, who shewed similar excitement. The Telegraph station was burnt down, and night after night the officer's bunglows were set on fire. Two days before the arrival of the 19th, an outbreak occured at Barrackpur. One Mangal Pande, calling upon his comrades, ordered the bugler to sound the assembly and fired his musket at a European Sergeant-Major. The native officer and men made no attempt to arrest him, but kept quiet. Lieutenant Baugh galloped to the spot, and Mangal Pande shot at him hitting his horse. Numbers of excited sepoys rushed up on hearing the firing. General Hearsey then approached, and Mangal Pande turned his piece upon himself and fell wounded. He was then secured and taken to hospital. The man recovered and both he and the officer in charge of the guard were tried by Court-Martial, condemned and hanged on the 8th and 22nd April respectively, in presence of all the troops. On the 31st March the 19th Regiment from Barhampur arrived, and the order of disbandment was carried out in the presence of all the troops, but not with disgrace, as they were penitent. The 34th was similarly disbanded but with disgrace.

Chittagong.—At this time, the 2nd, 3rd, and 4th Companies of the 34th Regiment Native Infantry were stationed at Chittagong. They were noted for their good conduct, and they expressed their desire to be sent to Delhi to act against the insurgent regiments. All on a sudden, on the night of the 14th November, 1857, they rose up, released all the prisoners from the jail, killed one *barkandas*, carried away all the treasure and left the station early next morning with three Government elephants, ammunition and treasure. On the 22nd November, they crossed the river Feni and entered the hills of the Raja of Hill Tipperah. The Raja arrested those who lingered behind, and sent them to the British authorities and they were executed. The amount of Government treasure taken by the mutineers was Rs. 2,78,267; of which only Rs 35,103 was recovered by the authorities of Sylhet and Cachar and Rs. 17,641 by the Magistrates of Chittagong and Tipperah.

Dacca.—On the 26th November, the news of the mutiny of the Sepoys stationed at Chittagong reached Dacca. There the Sepoys stationed were two companies of the 73rd Native Infantry. Before this, upon the arrival of the news of the outbreak at Meerut, an uneasy feeling manifested itself among the Dacca sepoys, and the Government sent a force of a hundred men of the Indian navy for the protection of the town. It was then thought proper that the Dacca sepoys should be disarmed. Perhaps they had been apprised of the intention, and were prepared to make resistance. The sentry fired his musket and killed a man. His example was followed by others, and a volley was fired on the sailors as they advanced. The sailors made a gallant charge and the sepoys took to flight. They concealed themselves in the jungles, and at last proceeded towards Maimansing and Sylhet; but several of the fugitives were captured, brought in, and executed.

In Behar, however, the mutiny took a formidable aspect, and the districts that suffered were Tirhut, Patna, Shahabad, Gya and Champaran.

Tirhut.—When the news arrived in June, that Delhi was in the hands of the insurgents, the English residents and better class of natives of Behar showed causes of anxiety. About the third week of that month, information was received by the authorities in Tirhut, that one Waris Ali, a police *Jamadar*, said to be of the blood royal of Delhi, was in treasonable correspondance with certain Muhammadans at Patna. Waris Ali was seized, taken to the station and hanged. On the following morning, the troops broke out into open mutiny. They attacked the Treasury and Jail but were driven off. They then shifted to Aliganj Sewan in Saran. No further outbreak took place in Tirhut.

Patna.—The sepoys stationed at Dinapur consisted of the 7th, 8th, and 40th Regiments of the Native infantry. The 7th and 8th Regiments openly revolted and were shortly joined by the 40th. The majority of the Sepoys took to the river Son, and were safe across in Shahabad. Here they found a leader by name Kuar Singh, of Jagadispur, a Rajput of much influence, nearly 80 years old.

Shahabad.—The rebel army, consisting of about 2000 sepoys and a multitude of armed insurgents four times as numerous, marched on Arrah. They reached the town on the 27th July, and forthwith released all the prisoners in the jail, and plundered the Treasury. The European women and children had already been sent away. The town was supplied with a garrison of fifty Sikhs, who held out for eight days, until rescued by Major Vincent Eyre on the 3rd August. The Major pursued the rebel chief up to his residence at Jagadispur. His stronghold was captured, and the grains he stored by taking forcibly from the villagers were re-distributed to them.

Gya.—When the news of the mutiny of the Dinapur sepoys reached Gya, the English residents grew apprehensive, and the Commissioner gave orders for their withdrawal into the city of Patna. All the other Europeans went to Patna, but the Magistrate Mr. Money secured the treasure consisting of 7 or 8 *laks* of rupees, took them to Calcutta by the Grand Trunk Road, as on all other sides there was apprehension of attack by the insurgents. He brought the treasure safe to Calcutta escorted by Captain Thompson and his party.

Champaran.—The fate of Champaran was different. The Twelfth Regiment of Irregular Horse was stationed at Sagauli, commanded by Major James Holmes. Up to the last he had full confidence in the fidelity of his men. One day in July, when he was taking his afternoon drive accompanied by his wife, he was attacked by a party of *Sawars* and butchered on the spot. At the sametime the remaining Europeans, including one little child, were also cut down. The regiment broke out into an open mutiny of the worst kind.

CHAPTER XII.

THE RULE OF THE BRITISH CROWN.

VICEROYS OF INDIA.	LT.-GOVERNORS OF BENGAL.
1858. Earl Canning.	1858. Sir Frederick Halliday.
1862. Earl of Elgin.	1859. Sir John Peter Grant.
1864. Sir John (Lord) Lawrence.	1862. Sir Cecil Beadon.
1869. Earl of Mayo.	1867. Sir William Grey.
1872. Earl of Northbrook.	1871. Sir George Campbell.
1876. Earl of Lytton.	1874. Sir Richard Temple.
1880. Marquis of Ripon.	1879. Sir Ashley Eden.
1884. Lord Dufferin.	1882. Sir Rivers Thompson.
	1887. Sir Steuart Bayley.

Sir Frederick Halliday—When the mutiny was suppressed, the Act for the better Government of India was passed in 1858. By it the administration was transferred from the Company to the Crown. It enacted that India shall be governed by, and in the name of, the Queen of England, through one of her principal Secretaries, assisted by a Council of fifteen members. The Governor-General received the title of Viceroy. On the 1st November, 1858, at a grand *darbar* held at Allahabad, it was announced that the Queen had assumed the Government of India. Peace was proclaimed throughout India on the 8th July, 1859.

The Covenanted Civil Service—At the sametime, the Covenanted Civil Service of India was thrown open to public competition, among all natural born subjects of her Majesty; and the natives of India were admitted into the service.

The Establishment of Sub-divisions—The events of the mutiny necessarily caused things to be a good deal thrown back. There was in the interior of Bengal, a state of lawlessness and high-handedness. The rich and the influential men took the law into their own hands by open violence, and the Lieutenant-Governor devoted his whole energy to put down this evil. One of the most important results of the measures taken was the establishment of the sub-divisions of districts, in each of which an officer was placed in charge with powers of Magistrate and some other powers. This system was most developed under the next Lieutenant-Governor Sir John Peter Grant. The Commissioner of Dacoity exerted his utmost to put down dacoity, which was prevalent in many districts of Bengal.

Coal in Bengal.—The existence of coal-mine in Bengal was discovered in 1774 by Mr. Heatly, who was at that time Collector of Chutia Nágpur and Palamow. It was actually worked in 1777. Mr. Jones first opened mines at Raniganj in 1815. In 1830 several collieries of considerable extent were flourishing. The coal tract now known as the Raniganj field extends from a few miles east of the town of Raniganj to several miles west of the Barakhar river, the greatest length from east to west being about thirty miles, and the greatest breadth from north to south about eighteen miles. A Geological survey was undertaken in 1845, and a thorough examination of the Raniganj coal-field was made by the Geological Department during 1858-60. There are, at present, also a few coal mines at work in the neighbouring districts of the Chutiá Nágpur Division.

Improvement of Bengali Literature.—The year 1859-60 witnessed a further development of the literature of the country. The old-school poet Isvar Chandra Gupta died, and Michael Madhu Sudan Datta appeared with his new form of poetry in blank verse. His *Tilottoma Shambhav Kabya* was first published in the *Rahashya Sandarvya* which was followed by his celebrated *Meghnadbadha Kabya*. The other two contemporary poets who achieved literary distinction are Babus Hem Chandra Bandyapadhyay and Rangalal Bandyapadbyay.

Sir John Peter Grant (1859—62.)—On the 2nd May, 1859 Sir John Peter Grant was appointed Lieutenant Governor of Bengal, in succession to Sir Frederick Halliday, who retired on the 1st of May, 1859. The provinces subject to the Lieutenant-Governor comprised at that time Bengal, Behar, and Orissa, Assam, Cachar, the Kasiah Hills, Arakan, the Chutiá Nágpur territory, and the part of Sikim attached to Darjiling. They produced one-third of the gross revenue of the Empire.

Administrative Changes—In 1859 the offices of Magistrate and Collector were again united. This reunion had been the subject of anxious deliberation in India for six years, before it was finally resolved upon. The measure was strongly advocated by Sir Frederick Halliday, by Lord Canning and was as strongly opposed by

Mr. Grant. It was sanctioned by Lord Stanley who was then the Secretary of State for India. At the sametime seven of the eight independent Joint-Magistracies already alluded to (see p. 155) were raised to full Magistracies and Collectorates. The district of Barasat was abolished and reduced to an ordinary sub-division.

A Dacoity Commission was established for Behar. A small gunboat was sent to cruise about in those Sundarban channels where the crime was most prevalent.

Zemindari Revolution.—The *Zemindars* with whom the permanent settlements had originally been made, were for the most part powerful men, whose authority extended over wide tracts of country, police and other powers being entrusted to them. Of these tracts they were by the settlement constituted the proprietors. But under the influence of debt and mismanagement, these large *Zemindaries* were speedily broken up. By the beginning of the present century, the greater portion of the estates of the Nadiya, Rajshahi Bishnupur, and Dinajpur Rajas had been alienated. The Bardwan estate was seriously crippled, and the Birbhum *Zemindari* was completely ruined. A host of smaller *Zemindars* shared the same fate. A complete revolution took place in the constitution and in the ownership of the estates.

Creation of Under-tenures.—The *Zemindars* for the internal management of their estates created in large numbers under-tenures known as *patni* tenures, and leased out extensive tracts on long terms. Dependent *taluks, gantis, haolas,* and other similar fixed and transferable under-tenures, existed before the settlement. In addition to all these, the former Governments, or the

Zemindars under those Governments, granted rent-free lands as religious endowments—grants which have since been recognised and confirmed by the English.

Rent Law of 1859.—The old law gave great powers to the *Zemindars*, with a view to enable them to realize their rents from the tenants. Under the *haftam* (seventh Regulation) process, the person of the ryot could be seized in default; under the *pancham* (fifth Regulation) process, his property could be distrained. The powers thus exercised by the *Zemindars* themselves, were reduced by the Rent Act of 1859. This Act while it afforded the remedy of a summary process, provided the grounds of enhancement. The rights of the ryots are at present more respected than they were; but on the other hand there is difficulty in quickly realizing undisputed rents by legal process.

Sale Law of 1859.—At the sametime, in order to secure the punctual payment of the Government revenue, the sale law of 1859 was passed. It is a very hard law. If the full revenue of an estate is not paid by sunset on the last day it is due, that estate at once becomes liable to sale for the arrear; and even if an estate has defaulted, either by accident or by misfortune, or by any other unfortunate cause, it is sold up, however small the arrear may be. This rigorous law has brought ruin on many *Zemindars* in Bengal. Many of the old aristocratic class have been reduced to insignificance, whereas men of inferior position in society, possessing money by trade or other means, have risen in the scale.

Railways.—The Eastern Bengal Railway Company was formed in 1857, and commenced actual operations in May, 1859. It runs from Calcutta to Goalanda in Faridpur District. The Calcutta and South-Eastern Railway Company was incorporated in 1857, and the actual work of constructing the line commenced in 1859-60.

Small Cause Courts.—The Small Cause Courts in Bengal were established by Sir John Peter Grant under Act XLII. of 1860.

The Hook-swinging.—The hook-swinging at the festival of the *Charak Puja* was suppressed by the use of the personal influence of the *Zemindars* and magistrates.

Kuki Raids.—At the beginning of 1860, the *Kukis*, hill tribes who dwell in the Chittagong Hills between the Karnafuli and the Fenny, left their mountain fastnesses and destroying the village of Ramghar, made a sudden descent on the plains of Tipperah. 187 persons were killed in the plains and 100 carried off as slaves. In the hills they killed about 300 persons and carried away 200 more into captivity. In the town of Commilla even serious apprehensions of an attack were for a time entertained. But the savages had no intention to face the attack of an organised body of troops. Before the military police had arrived upon the spot, the marauders had retired to the hills. In January, 1861, a force of military Police was sent against them and they were punished. The country was surveyed.

Rising of the Kasiahs.—This was followed by a rising among the Kasiahs of the Jiantia Hills, to the north of the District of Sylhet and adjoining Cachar on the west. This country came into British possession in 1835, when the Raja Raj Indra Sing voluntarily resigned his authority for a pension of 500 Rupees a month. In 1862 it was resolved to impose a house-tax on the country as a token of British authority. The people resisted, were punished and the tax was paid.

The Hill Tracts of Chittagong.—By Act XX of 1860, the portion of the country called the Hill Tracts of Chittagong consisting of 8200 square miles became a Non-regulation District. It was put in charge of a superintendent, who was at the same time Commandant of a Military Police Battalion, whose duty it was to guard the frontier.

Dealings with the Sikim Government.—In 1850, in consequence of the Raja of Sikim having seized and detained in confinement the Superintendent of Darjiling, the English took possession of the portion of Sikim lying to the west of the Great Ranjit and to the north of the Ruman River, and forfeited the allowance of the Maharaja. Towards the close of 1860, the Sikim authorities made constant raids on British territory. A military force was despatched, with the Hon'ble A. Eden as Envoy and Special Commissioner. They started for Darjiling on 1st February, 1861 and reached Tamlung, the Sikim capital, on 1st March. The Dewan who was the real author of all aggression fled ; the forts were dismantled and the old Raja abdicated in favour of his son, and on the 26th March a treaty was made with the new Raja on favourable terms. The allowance forfeited in 1850 was restored in 1862 as an "act of grace"; was increased to Rs. 9,000 in 1868, and to Rs. 12,000 in 1873 "on the understanding that it was granted without any reference to the increased value of Darjiling, and purely as a mark of consideration for the Maharaja."

The Indigo disturbances.—At this time occurred the indigo disturbances. Numerous applications from the ryots were received by the Bengal Government, complaining of cruel oppressions practised upon them by the indigo planters, and of the compulsory cultivation of a crop, which entailed on them harassing, vexatious and distasteful interference. A commission was appointed to enquire into the whole matter, and measures were taken to remedy the grievances of the ryots. Rai Dina Bandhu Mittra Bahadur published his famous *Nil-Darpan*, which created a great sensation at the time. It was translated into English and sent to England. Rev. Long who published the English version of the work was convicted by the Supreme Court and sentenced to imprisonment. The Hon'ble Seton Karr who helped in its circulation, and other civilians who were the friends and supporters of the natives against the indigo planters, incurred the odium of their non-official countrymen.

Criminal Law.—Many acts were passed during the administration of this Lieutenant Governor. Of these the most important were the Indian Penal Code, the Criminal Procedure Code and the Act for the Regulation of Police. The question of enacting a general Penal Code for India had long been under consideration. In 1837 it was completed by Lord Macaulay. In 1851 a revised edition was prepared by Mr. Bethune. It was further revised in 1856 and was passed into law on the 6th October, 1860. It came into force from 1st January, 1862. It superseded the Muhammadan law; and the employment of Muhammadan law officers in the Muffasil Courts was no longer necessary.

Creation of New Police.—In 1861 the Police was established as a separate department under the Magistrate; and District Superintendents and Assistant Superintendents of Police were appointed to discipline the force. An Inspector-General and Deputy Inspectors-General were placed at the head of the Police, to supervise and inspect the department.

Issue of Government Currency Notes.—On the 11th February, 1861 formal notice was served on the Banks of Bengal, Madras and Bombay, withdrawing from them the privilege of issuing notes. On the 1st March, 1862, Government Currency notes were first issued, through the agency of the three Presidency Banks.

Sir Cecil Beadon (1862-67.)—Sir Cecil Beadon succeeded Sir John Peter Grant as Lieutenant-Governor of Bengal on the 23rd April, 1862.

The Lieutenant-Governor's Council.—The Council of the Lieutenant-Governor of Bengal for the purpose of making Laws and Regulations was established in 1862 by the Governor-General in Council. The Lieutenant Governor is the President of the Council. He is empowered to nominate twelve councillors, not less than one-third of whom must be non-official members. The authority of the Council extends over all the provinces, districts and places which are administered by the Local Government; but before any law comes into force, it must have received the assent of the Governor-General of India as well as of the Lieutenant-Governor.

The Queen's coin.—By Act XIII of 1862 a new style of coinage was provided. The name of Her Majesty was substituted for the East India Company, and it was provided that the coins should bear a likeness of Her Majesty and the inscription Victoria Queen on the obverse and on the reverse the designation of the coin with the word India.

Money order offices.—Money order offices were established in Bengal in November, 1862.

Establishment of the High Court.—On the 14th May, 1862, the High Court of Judicature in Bengal was established by Letters Patent. The *Sadar* and Supreme Courts were abolished at the sametime. The combined powers and authorities of the abolished courts, and their jurisdictions, both over the provinces and the Presidency town, were vested in the High Court. On the 1st January, 1866, fresh Letters Patent were issued, and further provision was made respecting the jurisdiction of the Court. In respect of civil justice, the High Court of Calcutta exercises an appellate, a legal and equitable, an ecclesiastical, an admiralty, and a bankruptcy jurisdiction. The functions which in England have hitherto been divided among different courts, are here exercised in one Court and by the same judges. Qualified natives were permitted to be appointed as Judges of the High Court, and the Hon'ble Sambhu Nath Pandit was the first Bengali Judge appointed. He was followed by the Hon'ble Dwarka Nath Mittra, and the Hon'ble Anukul Chandra Mukhopadhyay.

M. A. Degree first conferred.—The degree of M. A. of the Calcutta University was in 1862-63 conferred for the first time.

Indigenous Schools.—Babu Bhudev Mukherji was

appointed Additional Inspector of Schools under the scheme devised by the late Lieutenant-Governor, for the improvement of indigenous schools, by the offer of money rewards to the *Gurus*. District Training Schools were opened for the training of village *Gurus*.

Kuch Behar State.—In 1863 a Commissioner was appointed for the Kuch Behar State, during the minority of the Raja. It is bounded on the north and west by the new district of Jalpaiguri; on the south by Rangpur; and on the east by the unsurveyed portion of the district as far as the Jaldoka and Tursa rivers. Its extreme length east and west is forty miles, and the extreme breadth north and south is thirty-six miles.

Nadiya and Bardwan Fever :—In 1863-64 an epidemic fever raged in the Nadiya and Bardwan districts, causing much mortality. Sanitary measures were enforced but failed. By some it was attributed to filth and overgrown jungle, by the others to obstructed drainage, but none of the proposed theories explains the mystery. Some considered that this was the same type of fever which three hundred years before devastated the old city of Gaur, and desolated Mahmudpur of Sita Ram in 1836.

Introduction of Municipalities.—The Municipal system has been introduced into provinces of Bengal from the year 1863. Twenty-six years ago, the town of Calcutta was governed by three men appointed by the Government, who managed all its affairs in municipal matters. By Act VI. (B. C.) of 1863 the municipal Government of the Town of Calcutta was vested in a Corporation under the title of "the Justices of the Peace for the Town of Calcutta." It came into operation on the 1st of July, 1863. Act III. (B. C.) of 1864, was passed by which large towns in the interior were regulated.

Agricultural Exhibition.—An Agricultural Exhibition was opened at Alipur on the 18th January, 1864. The articles exhibited were, Live Stock, Machinery and Implements and Produce. It remained open for a fortnight.

Cyclone of 1864.—On the 5th October, 1864, a great cyclone took place, which caused a terrible destruction of men, cattle, houses and property. Only 23 out of the 195 ships in the Hugli river escaped damage.

The District of Darjiling.—The portions of the hills known as British Bhutan, was ceded by the Bhutias after the Bhutia War in 1865, and annexed to Darjiling. The district was placed under the charge of an officer called Superintendent, whose designation has since been changed to that of Deputy Commissioner.

The Currency Department of Calcutta—The Currency Department was established in Calcutta, and from 1st January, 1866, the circulation of the Government Currency Notes has been made over to it.

The Famine of 1866—In the year 1866 Bengal was threatened with a severe scarcity. Prices of food grains increased week by week, till they rose to more than double the ordinary rates. It became apparent that absolute famine must ensue. The worst districts were the Cuttack Division (specially Puri) and Midnapur and the Behar Districts of Gya, Shahabad and Champaran, where there were great starvation and suffering and considerable mortality. A commission was appointed to inquire into the famine in Bengal and Orissa and much has been done to prevent the recurrence of a similar calamity.

Registration of deeds—The law for the registration of deeds was passed in 1866. A General Registry Office was established in Bengal and Registrars and Sub-Registrars, were appointed in the interior of the country.

Sir William Grey (1867—1871.)—Sir William Grey succeeded Sir Cecil Beadon as Lieutenant-Governor of Bengal on the 23rd April, 1867.

Appointment of Subordinate Judges.—In 1867 the judges of the Small Cause Courts and the Principal Sadar Amins and Munsifs were amalgamated into one service. Small Cause Court Judges and Principal Sadar Amins have since been called indifferently Subordinate Judges, and are eligible alike for Small Cause Court work or for the work of the ordinary Civil Court.

The East India Irrigation Company.—Orissa has from time immemorial been visited by terrible famines from draught. In the rainy season the rivers of the country devastate the plains, while they fail to yield a proper supply in summer. From long before it was in the comtemplation of Government to take measures against the recurrence of these calamities. In the year 1862 the East India Irrigation Company was started for the execution of necessary works for the irrigation of Orissa, and the protection of the country from floods. They were, however, unable to carry out their project to completion and on the 31st December, 1868, the Government took over the whole canal works from the Company at a cost of nearly 95 *laks* of rupees. The canals thus taken over from the Company and since completed are (1) The High-Level Canal, (2) The Kendrapara Canal, (3) The Taldanda Canal, and (4) the Machhgaon Canal with their respective distributaries.

The Orissa Canals.—The High Level Canal was designed to provide a navigable trade route between Cuttack, Baleshar, Midnapur and Calcutta and also to irrigate the country through which it passes; the Kendrapara Canal—to irrigate the high ground on the north or left bank of the Mahanadi, of the Chitartala and the Nun; the Taldanda Canal—to connect the city of Cuttack with the main branch of the Mohanadi within tidal range; the Machhgaon Canal—to connect Cuttack with the mouth of the Devi river. All the canals were proposed to keep on high levels.

South Behar Canals.—The project of irrigating South Behar, in the districts of Shahabad, Gya and Patna, by a comprehensive scheme of canals, which should also be navigable, dates from 1855. Active operations were commenced in 1869. It has also been proposed to extend it eventually to Mirzapur on one side and to Monghyr on the other. The works now consist of the Eastern Main Canal, the Patna Canal, the Western Main Canal, the Arrah Canal and the Buxar Canal. There can be little doubt that these canals have conferred upon South Behar an entire immunity from future famines.

Port Canning.—The idea of making a subsidiary port to Calcutta on the river Matla was started in 1853. In 1862 the Port Canning Municipality was formed. In

1865 the municipality succeeded in raising a debenture loan and the Port Canning Company which had been formed subscribed about 2½ laks of rupees. In March, 1866, the Government of India consented to a loan of 4½ laks of rupees on security of the property of the Municipality without interest, repayable in five years. The Company however failed and the rights of the municipality were purchased by the Government. Since then the port has been practically abandoned.

Visit of the Duke of Edinburgh.—Until this time no prince of the blood royal had ever set foot in India. The Duke of Edinburgh came in 1869 bearing messages of motherly love from the Sovereign to her people. His visit awakened chords which had lain mute since the overthrow of the Moghul dynasty. The people of Bengal gave a splendid reception to the Sailor Prince in Calcutta, such as had never been witnessed before.

Preliminary Census.—No regular census had ever been taken of Bengal. An experimental census was taken in some municipalities and towns in 1869, preliminary to the general census of 1871.

Retirement of Sir William Grey.—The Lieutenant-Governorship of Bengal was filled by Sir William Grey, till 1st March, 1871, when he made over the office to Mr. George Campbell.

Sir George Campbell (1871—74).—Sir George Campbell was called to preside over the administration of Bengal, from the rank and file of the service, without having filled the posts which usually lead to so great an office.

His administration—From the beginning he devoted his attention to the internal administration of the province. He made the District Officer the head of each district. In him he centralized all authority and made him the hand and eye of Government. He was made to control the working of all departments and bring it to a common action. To him the civil surgeon, the district superintendent of Police, the engineer, and a staff of assistants and deputies, exercising magisterial, executive, and revenue functions were all carefully subordinated. A new system of primary education for the masses was developed, the control and supervision of which he placed under him. A system of rural registration of deeds and documents was introduced and the district officer was made its head under the title of Registrar.

Census of 1871.—A census of the whole country in great detail was for the first time taken in 1871.

Assassination of the Viceroy and the Chief Justice.—The most striking and lamentable events in the beginning of the year 1872 were the unhappy assassinations of two of the greatest men in the country—the Viceroy Earl Mayo, and the officiating Chief Justice Norman. Both the assassins were Muhammadans of Afghanistan.

Character of the British Rule.—Yet it is a singular testimony to the stability of the British political system, that it does not depend on any man, however exalted and however able. The assassination of the Head of law did not cause the slightest appreciable variation in the value of the public funds in the Calcutta market, and the administration of the country proceeded in the usual way.

The Lushai Expedition.—In November, 1871, the Lushai expedition was undertaken to punish the serious raids committed by the frontier tribes called *Lushais* or *Kukis*, located in the country between the Chittagong Hill Tracts and Cachar. Two strong military columns under Brigadier-Generals Bourchier and Brownlow were organised and despatched from the Cachar and Chittagong sides respectively. Each column was accompanied by a political officer in order to conduct negotiations and assist the commanding officer with his advice and make the necessary arrangements for boats, provisions, coolies &c. The political officers deputed were Mr. J. W. Edgar c. I. E. and Captain Lewin. The expedition was highly successful. The northern column penetrated 193 miles from Cachar into the very heart of the Eastern Lushai country, reducing to submission the most powerful chiefs. The arms taken from the sepoys who had been killed last year were surrendered, the fine imposed on the tribe was paid, hostages accompanied the force on its return and guarantees were given for the free passage through the country in future of Government agents. The operations of the Chittagong column were equally successful. The Syloo and Howlong tribes made unreserved submission agreeing to surrender all their captives, abstain from raids, and give free passage to English messengers. The survey parties attached to each column succeeded in surveying topographically 6,500 square miles of new country.

The Garo Expedition.—In the Garo Hills, the independent tribes failed to give satisfaction for the murder of one of the survey establishment. Captain La Touche moved forward with a Police force to press for surrender of the murderers. The tribes surrendered and acknowledged British authority and engaged to pay tribute. But no sooner he turned his back, than they came down again, massacred a number of the subject Garos, and created much alarm even in the plains of Maimansing. They were repressed and the panic allayed and many geographical discoveries were made.

Road Cess Act of 1871.—It must be remembered that the lands of Bengal have never been valued, after detailed measurement, for the purpose of assessing land revenue. In order to provide a measure for this valuation, the Bengal Road Cess Act of 1871 was enacted. It has imposed rates on houses, mines and other immovable property which may in no case exceed one-half anna in each rupee of the net profits of the land-holders. The fund thus raised, is intended to construct and maintain the roads, canals and other means of communication in every district.

Pabna rent disturbances.—An unhappy result of the Road Cess Act was the rent disturbances of Pabna. The Zemindars attempted to consolidate the cesses with the rents, and to obtain at the same time large increase of rent. The ryots who have of late, learnt to show some independence of character and acquired some knowledge of their rights, united for a common action. Thus an extensive ryots' union was formed and rapidly spread. They circulated a report that the *Zemindars* were to be abolished and they were to be the Queen's ryots. Though there was no loss of life or very serious personal injury, there were serious breaches of the peace, a little plunder of property and some old quarrels were worked off. But peace was completely restored without military aid and the rioters were duly punished. The Lieutenant Governor issued a proclamation to warn the ryots against illegal action, while legal rights were recognised.

The Economic Museum.—In order to obtain an adequate knowledge of the products of the country the New Economic Museum was established in Calcutta.

A New System of Native Civil Service.—Sir George Campbell carried into effect the scheme for providing subordinate executive establishments under the Sub-divisional officers. The officers are called Sub-deputy Collectors and Kanongoes. He also introduced a system of special education and examination to fit a man for a career in the native civil service. He also pledged that promotion to the higher appointments should be made only from among the passed men of proved ability.

Bardwan and Hugli Fever.—In the year 1872, a terrible fever, causing much mortality, broke out again in Bardwan and Hugli, which gradually extended to Midnapur and Birbhum. The causes of the fever are still a mystery.

The flood of the Mahanadi.—A most disastrous flood occured in the Mahanadi in the rains of 1872, such as had never before been experienced. It lasted from the 28th June to the 7th July. The damage done to the irrigation works was nearly 5 *laks* of rupees.

The Educational Policy.—The new system of primary education for the masses was started and developed by Sir George Campbell. The teaching of Gymnastics in some of our Colleges and Schools was also introduced by him. He gave great encouragement to Muhammadan education. He was considered hostile to high English education among the natives and the Bengali language suffered a little at his hands.

The Famine of 1873.—Owing to the badly-distributed rainfall of 1873, there was a serious deficiency in the rice crop of that year. About the end of the year, matters assumed a gloomy aspect and some districts of Bengal and the whole province of Behar were threatened with famine. Sir George Campbell took early notice of the famine warnings, and devised measures to avert the threatening calamity. Early in the year 1873 he was associated with Sir Richard Temple in the administration of famine. The latter was deputed to Behar with full powers to direct and control the relief operations on the spot. In February 1874, Government relief became fairly established. Relief operations, in the shape of tank-digging, road-making, were opened; railways were commenced, embankments extended and large quantities of rice were imported. By the end of September the winter harvests and spring sowings were everywhere safe and the relief operations closed.

Retirement of Sir George Campbell.—In April 1874 Sir George Campbell retired from the Indian Service, with the view to enter upon a political career at home.

Sir Richard Temple (1874-1876.)—On the 8th April, 1874, Sir Richard Temple was appointed to succeed Sir George Campbell as Lieutenant Governor of Bengal.

Separation of Assam.—On the 7th of February, 1874 the province of Assam was separated from Bengal and created into a Chief Commissionership. Subsequently on the 17th of September, 1874, the district of Sylhet was also annexed to Assam.

Administrative Changes.—The policy of the Bengal Government to make the subdivision the unit of the administration was maintained and many new subdivisions were established. Changes were made in the boundaries of jurisdictions of established districts. Tirhut was divided into two districts, Mazaffarpur and Darbhanga. Murshidabad was transferred from the Rajshahi to the Presidency Division and the remaining six districts of the Rajshahi Division, as well as the districts of Darjiling, Jalpaiguri and Kuch Behar were formed into a new Commissionership, designated the 'Rajshahi and Kuch Behar Division.'

Special Census.—Immediately after the famine, a new census was taken in East Tirhut and in a part of the Sarun district (North Behar), which showed a population larger by 15 per cent. in the former and much the same as previously returned in the latter.

Statistical Reporter and Trade Statistics.—The monthly publication of the *Statistical Reporter* was sanctioned and maintained for sometime. The registration of the river-borne traffic was carried out in some riverside stations.

Destruction of Goalanda Terminus.—The Eastern Bengal railway was placed under a disadvantage owing to the destruction of its Goalanda terminus. The spur built up at a cost of nearly four *laks* of rupees for its projection was carried away by the stream of the Ganges. Much progress was made in the Northern Bengal State Railway.

Land Registration Act, 1876.—The maintenance of complete and authoritative register of all lands in the Province of Bengal, with the names and shares of the actual possessors, was considered to be of great convenience both to the Government, to the landed proprietors and to all classes of subordinate tenure-holders and ryots. Accordingly the new Land Registration Act was introduced. This measure became law in August, 1876, and all proprietors were required to register their names and interests within six months from the 1st November following.

Land revenue settlements.—In order to effect a settlement of lands not settled under the principle of the permanent settlement of Lord Cornwallis, many survey parties were employed in different parts of the Lower Provinces, during the years 1876 and following. The most important of them were *noabad* settlements of Chittagong, the settlement of the Government estate of Kharda in Orissa and the operations carried on in the Western Doars, the Darjiling Terai, and the temporarily-settled estates of Majnammutha and Jallamutha in Midnapur. In the Santal Parganahs, settlement operations were carried on for revised assessment and for fixity of tenure.

Cyclone and storm-wave of 1876.—On the night of the 31st October, 1876, a cyclone and storm-wave took place which devastated the south-eastern districts of Bengal. The districts of Bakargunj, Noakhali and the islands of Dakshin Sabazpur, Hatia and Sandwip suffered terribly. There were appalling destruction of life and property and serious injury done to the crops. The calamity was followed by a terrible outbreak of cholera, which caused a mortality even greater than that of the storm-wave itself. The total loss of life, directly and indirectly attributable to the cyclone, was nearly one and quarter *laks* of souls.

Visit of the Prince of Wales.—During the cold weather of 1875-76, Bengal was fortunate to welcome His Royal Highness the Prince of Wales. The visit of his Royal Highness created a sensation and interest in every part of Bengal and manifestations of loyalty were displayed by the splendour of his reception, and the eagerness with which the well-to-do portion of the native community of every part of Bengal, flocked to Calcutta to have a sight of the Prince. The Heir-Apparent's visit called forth a burst of passionate loyalty such as had never attended the progress of any Delhi Emperor.

Bengali Literature.—During the administration of this Lieutenant-Governor, the Bengali Vernacular literature and drama continued to flourish. *Tara Charit* or the biography of Tara Bai was written by a respectable native lady. An improved style, free on the one hand from a pedantic use of Sanskrit words, and yet on the other hand enriching the language by words from the parent Sanskrit, was established by the efforts of the more distinguished Bengali authors, especially by Babu Bankim Chandra Chattopadhyay. By the death of Mr. M. M. Datta and Rai Dina Bandhu Mittra Bahadur, Bengali literature suffered a great loss.

Deputation of Sir Richard Temple.—Early in January, 1877, Sir Richard Temple was deputed by the

Governor-General in Council on special duty to the distressed districts in the Madras and Bombay Presidencies, and the Hon'ble Ashley Eden was appointed to officiate as Lieutenant-Governor of Bengal.

Elective System in the Calcutta Municipality.—In 1863 the principle of associating a large number of the citizens, in the administration of the municipality of the town of Calcutta, was introduced by vesting the control in the hands of the justices. But all the justices were Government nominees, and so in theory it left the control as completely in the hands of the Government as before. In 1876 another step was taken, and the system of election was introduced.

Sir Ashley Eden (1877-1882).—Subsequently Sir Richard Temple having been appointed Governor of Bombay, Mr. Eden was confirmed in the Lieutenant-Governorship of Bengal with effect from 1st May, 1877.

The Empress of India.—The 1st of January, 1877 will be ever memorable in the annals of Indian administration, for the assumption of the title of the EMPRESS OF INDIA by Her Majesty the Queen. The ceremony was celebrated throughout Bengal by *darbars* held at the head quarters of each of the divisional Commissioners. The sum of Rs. 40,000 was granted by the Government of India for public rejoicings, which was supplemented by public contributions. 3,082 convicted prisoners in Bengal were released and partial remissions of their sentences were granted to 5,862 more. Sixty-four debtors were also released from the civil jails, the Government taking upon itself the responsibility of paying the claims for which they were detained, amounting to Rs. 3,389.

A certain number of convicts, undergoing sentences of transportation at Port Blair and other penal settlements, was also released. Certificates of honor were also distributed to those gentlemen who distinguished themselves by assisting in the administration, or otherwise rendered good service to Government.

Vernacular Press Act.—On the 14th March, 1878, the Vernacular Press Act was passed to improve the tone of the native press. This measure created a discontent among the educated natives, who are largely instrumental in the formation of public opinion.

Administrative Changes.—During the same year, the management of the affairs of the ex-King of Oudh and of the Mysore Princes was transferred to the Government of Bengal. The post of the Political Agent of Hill Tipperah was abolished, and a Native Assistant Political Agent was stationed at Agartola, subordinate to the Magistrate of Tipperah, who was made *ex-officio* Political Agent. The district of Maldah was transferred from the jurisdiction of the District and Sessions Judge of Dinajpur to that of the Sessions Judge of Rajshahi. In May 1879, Pabna and Bogra were formed into a judgeship with head quarters at Pabna.

The License Tax.—With a view to raise an additional revenue to meet charges necessary for the prevention and mitigation of famines, a license-tax on trades, dealings and industries was introduced. The minimum profits made liable to assessment were Rs. 250. Subsequently a new License Tax Act was passed, in which the minimum assessable income was fixed at Rs 500.

Kaithi Character.—Sir Ashley Eden substituted the

Kaithi for the Persian character in the local Courts and offices of Behar, which gave general satisfaction.

Statutory Civil Service.—The Supreme Government, in order to provide for the regular and periodical appointment of Natives of India to the Covenanted Civil Service under statute 33 Vic. chapter 3., issued a set of rules. Effect was given to them and the first appointment in the Statutory Civil Service was made in 1878.

Darjiling Tramway.—Under the patronage of Sir Ashley Eden, the Darjiling Tramway was commenced in April, 1879.

Bengali Additional Judge.—During the year 1879-80 an additional judgeship was created for the districts of Bardwan and Bankura and a Bengali sub-judge was selected for the post.

Deputation of Sir Ashley Eden.—Sir Ashley Eden having been selected to preside over the Commission appointed by the Supreme Government, to enquire into and report on the organization of the army in India, the office of the Lieutenant-Governor of Bengal was, during his absence from the middle of July to the commencement of December, 1879, filled by Sir Steuart. C. Bayley, Chief Commissioner of Assam, who retained also charge of the Assam administration.

The Police Gazette.—Early in the year 1880, the publication of the Police Gazette in three languages English, Bengali and Hindi was sanctioned and the departure of every professional thief is now notified in it.

The Bhutia Raid.—On the 20th March, 1880, a raid was made by a small band of Bhutias on a village in British territory, and one man, two women, and three children were carried off to Bhutan. Measures were at once taken to protect the villagers and it appeared from enquiries that the raid had been committed by private individuals in Bhutan. According to the treaty with Bhutan, Deb Raja was asked to arrest the raiders and surrender them to the British authority, as well as to restore the six persons taken away by them.

Census of 1881.—In 1881 a census was taken for Bengal, and though Assam formed no part of it now, the population increased since 1871 from 6,27,05,718 to 6,95,36,861 or 10·8 per cent.

Revision of the Educational Department.—During the administration of Sir Ashley Eden, the organization of the educational department was revised. The inspecting staff was strengthened by the appointment of Assistant Inspectors in the four largest circles. A graded system of appointment was for the first time introduced for the subordinate officers of the department.

Advancement of the People.—The Bengali literature and drama have continued to flourish beyond hope, and the cultivation of science made great strides. The English education has been largely extended and greatly improved. It has commenced to bear fruit. Authors and Scholars have multiplied who are of no mean repute. Many of the natives have raised themselves in all mental qualities to a level with the Englishmen. Many of them have occupied executive and judicial appointments and they have been found to discharge their duties with integrity and ability.

Postal Department.—Various measures for the improvement of the postal department were developed.

RULE OF THE BRITISH CROWN. 193

Post offices and receiving houses in the interior were multiplied, cheaper agents were employed for the charge of small offices and the system of rural delivery received further development and extension. The *Zemindari* post was organized on a satisfactory footing. On the 1st January, 1880, the money-order system was transferred from the treasuries to the post offices. Post-cards were also introduced to the great convenience of the general public.

Departure of Sir Ashley Eden.—Sir Ashley Eden held the reins of the Bengal Government for the full period of five years, the whole of which was marked by the financial and agricultural prosperity of the country. He left the shores of Bengal to join his appointment as a Member of the India Council.

Sir Rivers Thompson (1882-1886.)—Sir Rivers Thompson assumed office on the 24th April, 1881. It was during the first year of his administration that the provincial contract system was in force.

Lord Ripon's Reforms.—Lord Ripon was now the Viceroy of India, a man of grand liberal views, possessing a wide and sincere sympathy with the people of the country. Under his auspices, Bengal witnessed the introduction or development of changes of such administrative and financial importance, that it may fairly be said to have opened a new chapter in the history of Bengal. By repealing the Vernacular Press Act, he set free the native journals to make a free and fair discussion of public questions. His scheme of Local Self-Government gave a new political life to the natives of India. With a view to fit the people for the safe exercise of the rights he conferred, he appointed an Education Commission to take up measures in hand, to spread high education on a broader basis. Against the wishes of many Englishmen, he appointed the Hon'ble Ramesh Chandra Mittra to act as Chief Justice of the Calcutta High Court. He tried to equalize the native and the English races and to give the native Magistrates the jurisdiction over British born subjects. This was the origin of the celebrated Ilbert Bill agitation. The Englishmen displayed an universal exhibition of race insolence, and assumed attitude which is characterised by their dislike to the educated Bengalis. His Finance Minister Sir Evelyn Baring was also a man possessed of noble feelings, and of a heart bent upon doing good to the people. He took off the import duties on cotton goods and the whole import customs with few exceptions were abolished.

The Ilbert Bill Agitation.—During the Ilbert bill agitation, Sir Rivers Thompson sided with his own countrymen, and became unpopular with the natives of the country.

Straitened Condition of the people.—The five years of plenty, which marked the rule of Sir Ashley Eden, were followed by three years in succession of scanty and uneven rainfall. Though there had been no actual distress, in many districts the resources of the poorer classes were wholly exhausted and their circumstances became straitened.

Executive Reforms.—Sir Rivers Thompson created a new department by the name of Agricultural Department. He published the rules for the admission of the natives of Bengal to the higher grades of the Opium Department. The elective system was introduced into municipalities, and the provisions of local self-government were extended to a large portion of the Province. District and Local Boards were established, having powers and duties in many matters of public interest and utility. A system of public examination was introduced to fill up vacancies in the Statutory Civil Service and in the Subordinate Executive Service.

Kuch Behar State made over.—The State of Kuch Behar, which had been under the administration of the Bengal Government for a period of about 20 years, was given over to the charge of Maharaja Nripendra Narayan Bhup Bahadur, on his attaining majority in October, 1883.

Calcutta International Exhibition.—In the year 1883-84 an international exhibition was held in Calcutta. It was the first undertaking of its kind in India. It was opened by Lord Ripon on the 4th December, 1883, and was closed also by the same viceroy on the 10th March, 1884. This Exhibition was no doubt, instrumental in spreading a wider knowledge of the raw products of India among the manufacturers of Europe and Australia, and in acquainting the population of this country with the capabilities of European machinery, but the country itself does not seem to be benefited by it. The manufactures of the country will still more decay, if the people depend on European manufacturers and do not learn to produce them in the country.

The Bengal Tenancy Act.—The Bengal Tenancy Act came into operation in 1885. The object of the

Act is to prevent too great a rise in rents. It recognises the rights of the cultivators in the soil which they have long tilled, and the rents of such hereditary tenants cannot be raised above fair rates fixed by the Courts. Within a hundred years the demand of land has increased so much, and the number of cultivators has grown so large, that in some districts they will offer any rent for a piece of ground. Formerly the landlords had to tempt husbandmen to settle on their estates, by giving them land at low rates, and sometimes by allowing them additional expenses for their cattle and plough or the costs for raising their houses. At present the manufacturers and artizans of the country, failing to compete with the superior productions of the European Machinery, have recourse to cultivation. Thus the general mass of the people of Bengal have turned agriculturists who are solely to depend on the produce of the land. During the year 1886, the cadastral survey and settlement operations under the Act were undertaken in the Muzaffarpur district as an experimental measure.

Railway Extensions.—Within the last thirty years many railway extensions have been effected throughout the province, providing easy mode of communication to the people. The East Indian Railway, which connects Bengal with the Upper Provinces, is now the property of the Imperial Government, and is worked through the agency of a company. The Eastern Bengal Railway, between Calcutta and Goalanda, lapsed to the Government of India in 1884, having previously been the property of a company. The Calcutta and South-Eastern Railway is also the property of Government. The

Patna Gya Railway though a Government line, has hitherto been worked through the agency of the East Indian Railway Company. The Bengal Central, Bengal and North-Western, Tarakeswar, Darjiling-Himalayan and Deogarh lines are the property of limited liability companies. A branch of the East Indian Railway has been opened from Bankipur to the bank of the Ganges at Digha Ghat. The Hugli River has been crossed at Naihati by a bridge, connecting the East Indian and Eastern Bengal Railways. Diamond Harbour, which may be considered as the actual mouth of the Hugli has been connected with Calcutta by a branch of the Calcutta and South-Eastern Railway. An entirely new line has been constructed, connecting Narainganj, Dacca and Maimansingh. A swift railway steamer now runs between Narainganj and Goalanda. The Assam coolie traffic has been greatly facilitated by the construction of the Kauniya-Dharla line. The Tirhut System has been extended in three directions throughout the districts of Darbhanga and Champaran. The Assam-Behar system is an extension of the Northern Bengal System of metre gauge railways into the Purniah and Dinajpur districts, and will, when completed bring Behar and Western Bengal into direct communication *via* Sahibganj on the East Indian Railway with Darjiling and Assam.

Postal and Telegraphic System.—The postal system considerably developed, and in order to give telegraphic facilities to the people, combined post and telegraphic offices were opened in different parts of the province.

Stamp Revenue.—The administration of the stamp duty is an important source of revenue. . The levy of it dates from 1797. The original measure was a small matter, its object being to provide for the deficiency occasioned in the public revenue by the abolition of the Police tax. It has gone on expanding. From a yield of 22 *laks* in 1840-41 it rose in rapid strides to about 31 *laks* in 1859-60 and to 130 *laks* in 1884-85. The later development of the revenue being due to the operation of the Indian Stamp Act of 1879 and the Court Fees Act of 1870.

Political Revolution.—Mr. Lal Mohan Ghosh went to England, and stood as a liberal candidate for the representation of the Deptford borough, in order to secure a seat in Parliament. Though ultimately he failed to enter Parliament, he paved the way for the future leaders of the country and opened the door for a political revolution now taking place in India.

National Congress.—About the end of 1886, the second National Congress was held in Calcutta. The object of the Congress is to do good, substantial, and solid work for the benefit of our common country. Whether any immediate good comes from the Congress or not, it has afforded an opportunity for the meeting of the best intellects and best hearts among our countrymen in various parts of India. The glorious indication of the National Congress is, that people of all parts of India have combined with a common purpose of improving the welfare of the mother country.

Loss of Bengali Literary men.—During the last five years almost all the distinguished men who laboured

www.ingramcontent.com/pod-product-compliance
Lightning Source LLC
Chambersburg PA
CBHW020910230426
43666CB00008B/1400